RAINCOAST CHRONICLES 24

JUDITH WILLIAMS · RAINCOAST CHRONICLES 24

Cougar Companions

BUTE INLET COUNTRY AND THE LEGENDARY SCHNARRS

Judith Williams

for Sandrine & Tess

Happy Birthday

1 2 3 4 5 — 23 22 21 20 19

Harbour Publishing Co. Ltd.
P.O. Box 219, Madeira Park, BC, V0N 2H0
www.harbourpublishing.com

All maps by Roger Handling except the maps on pages 43 and 78
Edited by Audrey McClellan
Indexed by Michelle Chiang
Cover design by Anna Comfort O'Keeffe
Text design by Roger Handling
Front cover photo: Unknown commercial photographer. Image MCR 15626 courtesy of the Museum at Campbell River
Back cover photo: August Schnarr photo. Image MCR 20447-20 courtesy of the Museum at Campbell River
Printed and bound in Canada

Canada Council for the Arts | Conseil des Arts du Canada

Canada

Harbour Publishing acknowledges the support of the Canada Council for the Arts, which last year invested $153 million to bring the arts to Canadians throughout the country.

Nous remercions le Conseil des arts du Canada de son soutien. L'an dernier, le Conseil a investi 153 millions de dollars pour mettre de l'art dans la vie des Canadiennes et des Canadiens de tout le pays.

We also gratefully acknowledge financial support from the Government of Canada and from the Province of British Columbia through the BC Arts Council and the Book Publishing Tax Credit.

Library and Archives Canada Cataloguing in Publication

Title: Raincoast chronicles 24 : cougar companions : Bute Inlet Country and the legendary Schnarrs / Judith Williams.

Other titles: Cougar companions

Names: Williams, Judith, 1940- author.

Description: Includes index.

Identifiers: Canadiana (print) 20190063726 | Canadiana (ebook) 20190063734 | ISBN 9781550178623 (softcover) | ISBN 9781550178630 (HTML)

Subjects: LCSH: Schnarr, August, 1886-1981. | LCSH: Inlets—British Columbia—Pacific Coast—Pictorial works. | LCSH: Pacific Coast (B.C.)—History. | LCSH: Pacific Coast (B.C.)—History—Pictorial works.

Classification: LCC FC3845.B87 W54 2019 | DDC 971.1/1—dc23

Table of Contents

Acknowledgements

Cougar Companions was developed with the generous help of Glen Macklin; Pearl Schnarr Macklin; Glen, Helen, Norman and Albert Fair; and Homalco Chief Darren Blaney. Marion Schnarr Parker compiled Pearl Schnarr's *Cougar Companions* album, which Christa Ma loaned me. Sylvia Rasmussen Ives, Rita Rasmussen, Vern Logan, Rolf and Heather Kellerhals, Randy Bouchard, Dorothy Kennedy and Mike Moore contributed important information and photos. Thanks to Bonnie MacDonald and the Cortes Island Museum and Archives Board and volunteers, and Sandra Parish, director of the Campbell River Museum and Archives, for the opportunity to mount *Naming and Claiming: The Creation of Bute Inlet*, where Schnarr photographic material was first exhibited.

My husband, Robert (Bobo) Fraser, was my companion on all Bute Inlet expeditions. In 1991 the late Sam Smythe drove us deep up into the Homathko Valley. Chuck and Sheron Burchill made our later Homathko Camp and Bute visits rewarding in every way. John and Cathy Campbell helped us collect waterway samples and navigate the Southgate River.

I greatly appreciate Audrey McClellan's thoughtful editing of a third manuscript of mine.

Opposite: Pearl Schnarr and Girlie. *Unknown commercial photographer. Image MCR 15626 courtesy of the Museum at Campbell River*

Bute Inlet from the alpine to Fawn Bluff, 1925. *August Schnarr photo. Image MCR 14399 courtesy of the Museum at Campbell River*

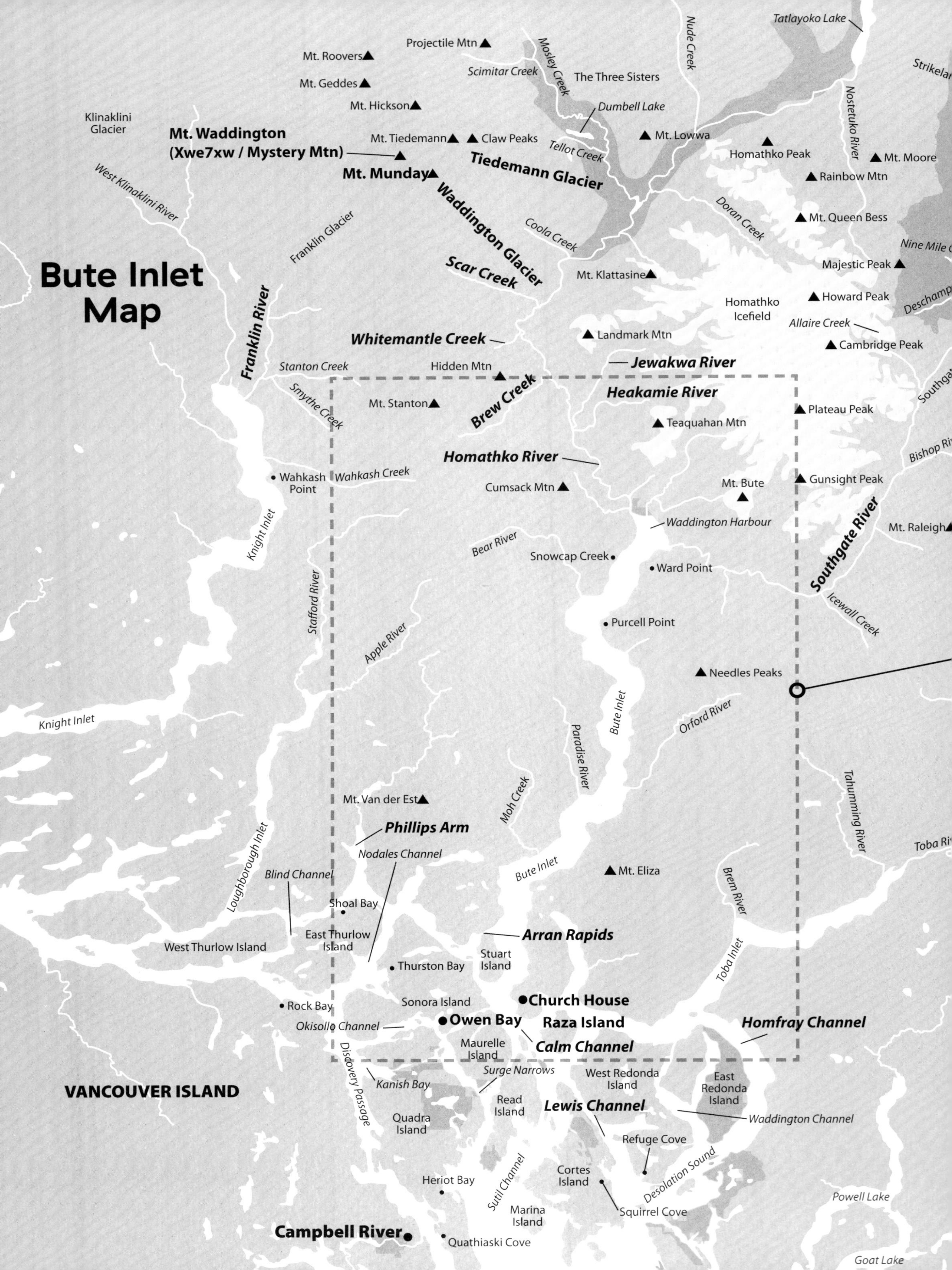

Bute Inlet Map
Mt. Roovers
Projectile Mtn
Mt. Geddes
Mt. Hickson
Scimitar Creek
Mosley Creek
The Three Sisters
Nude Creek
Tatlayoko Lake
Dumbell Lake
Klinaklini Glacier
Mt. Waddington (Xwe7xw / Mystery Mtn)
Mt. Tiedemann
Claw Peaks
Tellot Creek
Mt. Lowwa
Homathko Peak
Nostetuko River
Mt. Moore
Tiedemann Glacier
Rainbow Mtn
Mt. Munday
West Klinaklini River
Waddington Glacier
Franklin Glacier
Coola Creek
Doran Creek
Mt. Queen Bess
Scar Creek
Mt. Klattasine
Majestic Peak
Howard Peak
Homathko Icefield
Allaire Creek
Franklin River
Whitemantle Creek
Landmark Mtn
Cambridge Peak
Stanton Creek
Hidden Mtn
Jewakwa River
Heakamie River
Smythe Creek
Mt. Stanton
Brew Creek
Plateau Peak
Teaquahan Mtn
Homathko River
Wahkash Point
Wahkash Creek
Cumsack Mtn
Mt. Bute
Gunsight Peak
Waddington Harbour
Mt. Raleigh
Southgate River
Knight Inlet
Bear River
Snowcap Creek
Ward Point
Stafford River
Icewall Creek
Purcell Point
Apple River
Needles Peaks
Knight Inlet
Bute Inlet
Orford River
Paradise River
Moh Creek
Tahumming River
Mt. Van der Est
Phillips Arm
Nodales Channel
Loughborough Inlet
Blind Channel
Bute Inlet
Mt. Eliza
Brem River
Shoal Bay
East Thurlow Island
West Thurlow Island
Arran Rapids
Stuart Island
Thurston Bay
Toba Inlet
Rock Bay
Sonora Island
Church House
Owen Bay
Raza Island
Homfray Channel
Okisollo Channel
Maurelle Island
Calm Channel
Discovery Passage
Surge Narrows
West Redonda Island
East Redonda Island
Kanish Bay
VANCOUVER ISLAND
Read Island
Lewis Channel
Waddington Channel
Quadra Island
Refuge Cove
Cortes Island
Desolation Sound
Heriot Bay
Sutil Channel
Powell Lake
Marina Island
Squirrel Cove
Campbell River
Quathiaski Cove
Goat Lake

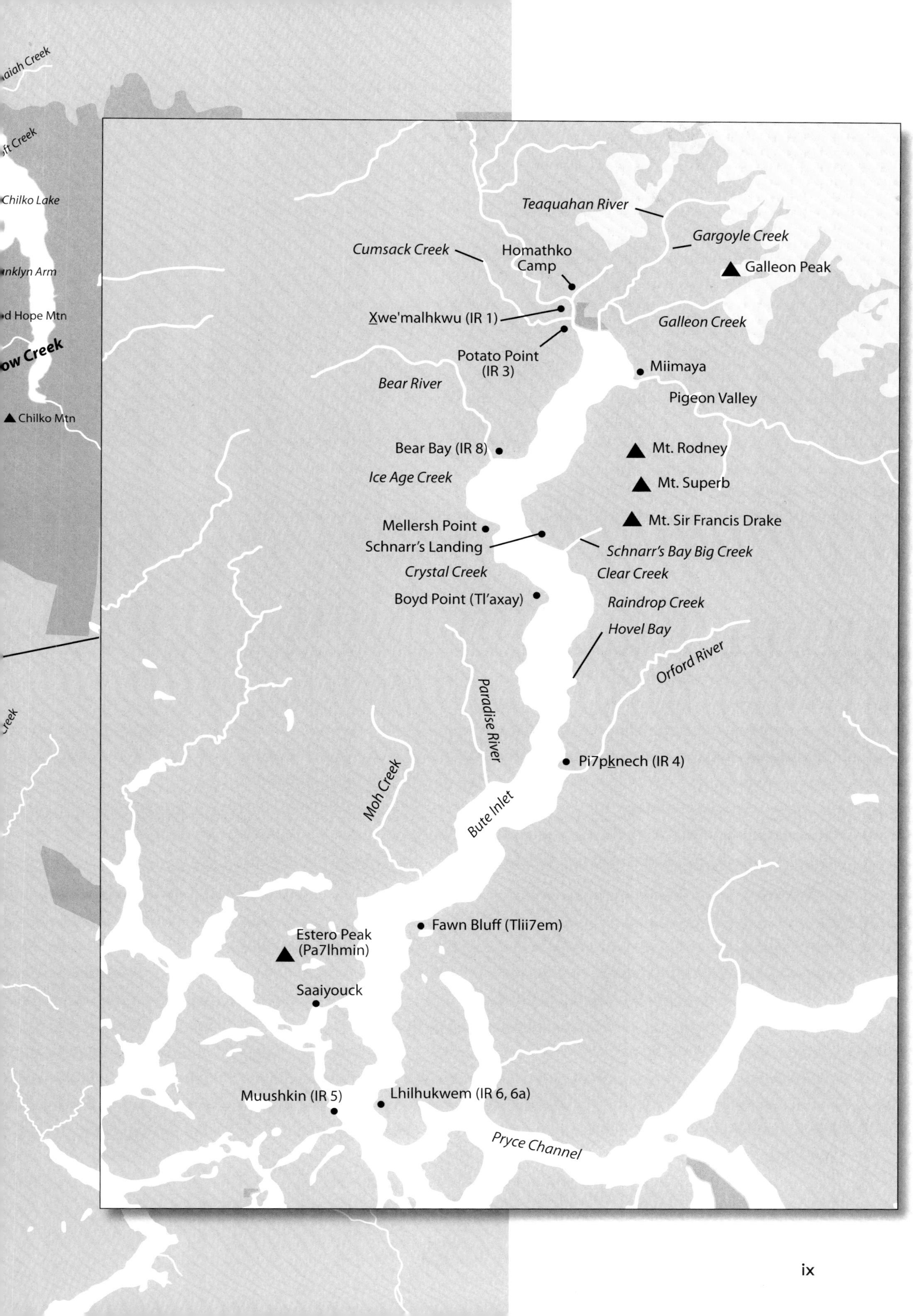

aiah Creek
ft Creek
Chilko Lake
nklyn Arm
d Hope Mtn
ow Creek
Chilko Mtn
reek

Teaquahan River
Gargoyle Creek
Cumsack Creek
Homathko Camp
Galleon Peak
Xwe'malhkwu (IR 1)
Galleon Creek
Potato Point (IR 3)
Miimaya
Bear River
Pigeon Valley
Bear Bay (IR 8)
Mt. Rodney
Ice Age Creek
Mt. Superb
Mt. Sir Francis Drake
Mellersh Point
Schnarr's Landing
Schnarr's Bay Big Creek
Crystal Creek
Clear Creek
Boyd Point (Tl'axay)
Raindrop Creek
Hovel Bay
Orford River
Paradise River
Pi7pknech (IR 4)
Moh Creek
Bute Inlet
Fawn Bluff (Tlii7em)
Estero Peak (Pa7lhmin)
Saaiyouck
Muushkin (IR 5)
Lhilhukwem (IR 6, 6a)
Pryce Channel

INTRODUCTION
SCHNARR'S LANDING

Of the settlers, prospectors, trappers, mountaineers and loggers who came to British Columbia's remote Bute Inlet between the 1890s and the 1940s, few remained long. August Schnarr trapped far up the Homathko and Southgate Rivers and logged the inlet shores from 1910 until the 1960s. His knowledge of the waterways, their navigation and the routes up their valleys to the Interior earned him a reputation as a legendary woodsman. An adventurous photographer, August carried his Kodak camera up the 80-kilometre (50-mile) inlet with the surrounding mountains rising to 2,750 metres (9,000 feet) around him. He strapped the camera to his suspenders during upriver treks into the alpine areas few dared traverse and documented his homesteading and logging achievements. Schnarr's photo collection is a diary of fifty years of an upcoast working life.

Opposite: August Schnarr in front of the "Grizzly" ice formation, at the foot of Klinaklini Glacier, with his Kodak camera case hooked on his suspenders, c. 1913. *"Water Power Investigations: Report on Taseko–Chilko–Homatho project," page 1243, photo 74*[1]

August, born in 1886, was the eldest son of a German-American family of three boys and a girl, Minnie, who settled in Centralia, Washington state. They built a log house in big fir country, cleared land by burning the trees down, and farmed and hunted for a living.

"You worked from the time you was able," August told Campbell River Museum interviewers Joan Skogan and Jan Havelaar in 1977. "Well, of course, living in a place like that you had nothing but woodlot around you [and] I got interested in animals, trapping. And about the only things I had around there was coon . . . You had to do something you know, and so I got this and that. Then I got to hearing about British Columbia. I was in Gastown in 1907 and the whole of Vancouver was Water Street, Pender and Hastings Street. That's all that was there. They were logging . . . Well, in 1909 I came back again and I been here ever since."[2]

Steam donkey in Hovel Bay, Bute Inlet, 2017.
Glen Macklin photo

August rowed up from the United States in a 16-foot double-ended open boat, logged at Port Harvey on Cracroft Island in 1910, then explored Knight Inlet and fished along the coast into Bute Inlet with his brothers Gustave (Gus) and Johnny when logging shut down for the season. In order to continue exploring the wilderness that had captured his spirit, August became a handlogger, hunter, trapper and boat builder in the Shoal Bay area. By the mid-1920s he and his wife, Zaida, had moved their floathouse into Bute and were raising their daughters, Pansy, Pearl and Marion, at what came to be called Schnarr's Landing, two-thirds of the way up the inlet.

Bute is the second longest of the series of fiords that poke crooked fingers into the northwest coast of North America. It averages 3.7 kilometres (2 miles) in width and descends to a depth of 650 metres (2,132 feet). Captain George Vancouver named the inlet after John Stuart, the third Lord Bute, whose grandson Charles Stuart was aboard Vancouver's ship *Discovery* during his 1792 exploration of the BC coast.

From 1926, pioneering Coast Range mountaineers Don and Phyllis Munday, inspired by Bute's vast unexplored mountains, used August's local knowledge and the trapping cabins he had built up the Homathko Valley for the first assault on 4,019-metre (13,186-foot) Mt. Waddington, the highest mountain completely within British Columbia. Hydraulic engineer F.W. Knewstubb, apprised of August's woodcraft, employed him to guide a BC government survey party examining the hydroelectric potential of Bute's rivers in 1928–30.

Once such doughty coastal adventurers are gone and the wilderness fills in their tracks, what is left? Perhaps a moss-laden roof composting down in an alder grove surrounding a rusted-out "steam donkey"—used to haul logs from the woods. And if a writer is lucky, an articulate descendant will pull from a drawer a family album containing a photo of that steam donkey in action.

Since their invention, photographs have been mined long after they were snapped for social data, point of view and an atmosphere intended or felt by a viewer from a different time and place. Whether candid or staged, they become half of what we can know and use to picture and colour past lives. The cornucopia of photos, negatives, interviews and household ephemera donated by

Steam donkey, 1920s. The tiny man to the left of the donkey, beside August's overturned dugout canoe, provides scale.
August Schnarr photo. Image MCR 20447-17 courtesy of the Museum at Campbell River

the Schnarr family to the Campbell River Museum and Archives has provided remarkably informative and reverie-inducing material for an exploration of the Schnarrs' lives and has led me up the Bute river valleys that have fascinated and occasionally consumed other travellers.

Why did August, a self-educated, hard-labouring and prickly character, purchase a camera and source film and its processing from his remote location? Why make such an effort to picture his world? Talking to his family, friends and adversaries, one gets a sense that August *owned* "Bute," which stood for this wide-ranging world in which he was more at home and with which he was more enduringly engaged than most other residents and explorers. His careful imaging of the very activities needed to earn a living within that landscape—moving a float camp or cutting down a huge tree by himself—seemed to satisfy an aesthetic, ego-gratifying or even spiritual need I am sure he would not have described as such.

For a viewer schooled to value and to parse a photo for motivation, composition, social import and documentary value, a significant selection of the Schnarr photo collection allows for extended "readings." Social documents in the broadest sense of the word, when combined with the Schnarr ephemera in the Campbell River Museum Archives they allow exploration of the skills demanded for this bone-crushingly hard life and the complexity of a pioneering coastal character that could sustain it. Gratifyingly, the Schnarr images often reveal that daily life with an unstudied beauty of composition and mood. The mountaineering Mundays and the hydro survey crew produced stunning images of the mountain splendour they all moved through, but they tell us nothing of residing *in* grandeur, raising pet cougars and earning a living in the Coast Range while continuing to be awed by the surroundings, as August most determinedly does. *Look*, he says, turning from the icy "Grizzly" to us. *Look at THAT!* August's photos are love letters to the northwest Pacific Coast.

PROLOGUE

COUGAR COMPANIONS

THE GOOD PHOTOGRAPH IS NOT THE OBJECT, THE CONSEQUENCES OF THE PHOTOGRAPH ARE THE OBJECTS.

—DOROTHEA LANGE

Fall 2010

He was angry. On the phone, in silences between half sentences, I heard his laboured breathing.

I got his name wrong at first: "Ben?"

"I'm Glen," he said. "Glen Macklin, Pearl Schnarr's son."

Several years earlier I'd met August Schnarr's grandson Glen Fair on a fishboat in Doctor Bay. "Ever read a book called *High Slack* about Bute Inlet?" that Glen had asked.

Marion, Pansy and Pearl with cougars Leo and Girlie. From Pearl Schnarr's *Cougar Companions* album.
Image MCR 2006-8 courtesy of the Museum at Campbell River

There was an awkward pause. "I wrote it," I said.

"Well," he continued, not missing a beat, "I'm the son of Pansy Schnarr, one of the sisters who had the cougars as pets up there."

Had August's oldest daughter, Pansy, and second daughter, Pearl, both named their sons Glen? The one now on the phone, the angry one, had to be Glen #2. I listened, said nothing, until I finally realized he was angry about the *Cougar Companions* photo album a friend had loaned me for my research on a Bute Inlet project for the Cortes Island Museum. She had said it belonged to Glen.

"I called Glen Fair," I said. "He gave me permission."

"It's not his, he's not part of the family," the phone voice said.

I was puzzled. Then I remembered Glen Fair had said his mother, Pansy, was not August Schnarr's daughter. "No, she was not," he'd repeated as if it was a new idea.

"He's not a member of this family," said Glen #2. "He gave the album to the museum. I had to fight to get it back. They kept the old photos—well, they're better there, but . . ."

Now I wasn't sure who to give the album back to. What had happened?

"I wanted to copy some of the photos," I said.

"No."

"I haven't copied anything yet."

"Good. You see, there's three albums made by Aunt Marion," Glen #2 said, "each different. This one you have is Pearl's, my mom's."

Above left: ***Cougar Companions*** **album cover.**
Image MCR 2006-8 courtesy of the Museum at Campbell River

Above right: ***Cougar Companions*** **album page.**
Image MCR 2006-8 courtesy of the Museum at Campbell River

As he explained more, and my long fascination with the inlet reached him, his tone changed. He was still angry, but his voice softened, became interested.

"I want to meet you," he said.

Marion Schnarr Parker made three *Cougar Companions* albums, for her sisters, Pansy and Pearl, and her father, August Schnarr. As I turned the pages of Pearl's album in 2010, August's magnificent landscape photos made it easy to slide up the liquid spine of Bute Inlet into a coastal history that paralleled my mother's 1917–1930s Texada Island childhood and my early experiences there in the 1940s. Men held fish up to be photographed. People posed on wooden gasboats nudging log booms. Houses were towed across water, and a woman holding a child leaned against a rock by the sea and laughed. But the album's startling 1930s pictures of the Schnarr girls with their pet cougars opened a very singular track to the past.

After Glen Macklin demanded I return Pearl's album, he took me to hand it back to her. She wanted to tell her story, and together they helped me follow the family tracks through the inlet I had previously explored for its violent 1860s history.

I was first captivated by Bute Inlet in the 1990s, when I travelled up the inlet to collect material for *High Slack*, a visual art installation at the UBC Museum of Anthropology that evolved into a book. Both centred on events in the inlet during the 1860s, when entrepreneur Alfred Waddington, abed with gout, a ruler and a rough map, conceived a plan to build a toll road up the Homathko Valley at the end of Bute Inlet to Interior goldfields in Tŝilhqot'in territory. Giving little thought to climate and topography, and none to the inlet's Indigenous inhabitants, he sent Royal Engineer Robert Homfray to do a survey for the road in the winter of 1861. Suppressing Homfray's reports of Bute's mercurial wind and temperature fluctuations, an attack by hostile Tŝilhqot'in, the loss of his canoe in the rampaging Homathko River, and his stranded crew's rescue and return to Victoria engineered by a Klahoose chief, Waddington started road construction the following year.

When August Schnarr explored and trapped up through the same territory, he searched for and photographed evidence of that road and the killing of the road crew by Tŝilhqot'in warriors who, responding to a threat to infect them with smallpox, declared war on the intruders. The People of the River, now known as the Tŝilhqot'in National Government, still maintain that the abuse of women also contributed to their decision to attack the interlopers, and they demand a pardon for the men the BC government hunted, duplicitously captured and hanged.[3]

August's daughters, the strong-faced young women in *Cougar Companions*, hugged their cougars, built boats, towed logs, photographed their party dresses and created a life in the wilderness in which they found themselves. Fascinated by these images, I wanted to learn every detail of the Schnarr sisters' domestic, private and working lives, and their unique experience raising the big cats. How had the 1930s media attention and representation of handsome cougars attended by attractive girls affected their view of themselves? And once the album photos made me aware of the extent to which August had documented his life from 1913, I parsed the photographs for clues to his life-defining bond with the inlet geography and history that I share. The album was the key to a clock, allowing me to rewind time.

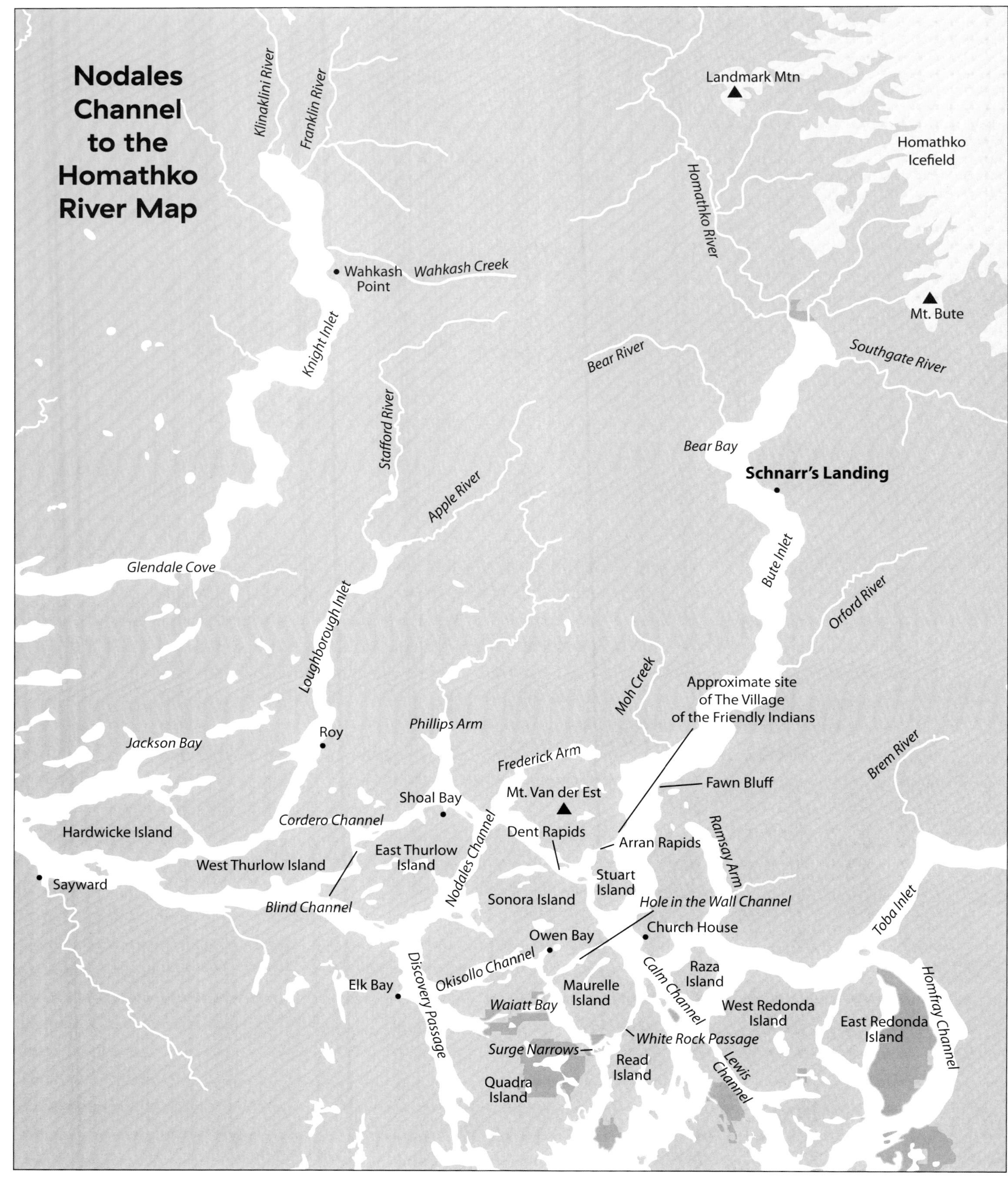
Nodales Channel to the Homathko River Map
Klinaklini River
Franklin River
Landmark Mtn
Homathko Icefield
Homathko River
Wahkash Point
Wahkash Creek
Mt. Bute
Knight Inlet
Southgate River
Bear River
Stafford River
Bear Bay
Schnarr's Landing
Apple River
Glendale Cove
Bute Inlet
Orford River
Loughborough Inlet
Moh Creek
Approximate site of The Village of the Friendly Indians
Phillips Arm
Roy
Jackson Bay
Brem River
Frederick Arm
Fawn Bluff
Shoal Bay
Mt. Van der Est
Cordero Channel
Hardwicke Island
Dent Rapids
Arran Rapids
Ramsay Arm
East Thurlow Island
Nodales Channel
West Thurlow Island
Stuart Island
Sayward
Sonora Island
Blind Channel
Hole in the Wall Channel
Toba Inlet
Church House
Owen Bay
Okisollo Channel
Raza Island
Calm Channel
Elk Bay
Discovery Passage
Maurelle Island
Homfray Channel
Waiatt Bay
West Redonda Island
East Redonda Island
White Rock Passage
Surge Narrows
Read Island
Lewis Channel
Quadra Island

1

MEMORY AS THEATRE

MEMORY IS NOT AN INSTRUMENT FOR SURVEYING THE PAST BUT ITS THEATRE.
—WALTER BENJAMIN, *BERLIN CHILDHOOD*

Glen Macklin was late.

"Boat ran out of gas out in the saltchuck last night," he said as he opened the pickup door. "Slept in."

We drove up from Heriot Bay, where August Schnarr had moved his floathouse when he left Bute in the '60s, and turned onto Macklin Road. Glen parked next to a swath of grass decorated with a wooden propeller that he said August had carved to drive his canoe up the Homathko River.

August Schnarr's wooden propeller and metal stand.
Judith Williams photo

Upstairs in the bungalow, his mother, Pearl Myrtle Schnarr Macklin, crept from the living room to sit at a chrome kitchen table by a window overlooking the lawn. Her sweet face was framed by long grey hair tied back in a girlish way, her spine twisted by osteoarthritis.

Pearl was eighty-three and she was tired. She rested one hand on a pile of old photo albums she had assembled for me, slid over a smaller one given to August by the mountaineering Mundays he had guided, and opened the *Cougar Companions* I handed back to her.

"My album, with pictures from our childhood," she said. "I still have the camera he took everywhere. Here's my mother, Zaida."

Merry-faced Zaida stands behind Pansy in a cedar-stake-fenced yard. August holds baby Pearl, born in 1923. On January 5, 1922, August had married Zaida May Lansall from Thurston Bay on Sonora Island, where settlers from Ontario had been given land. Pansy was born in its inner bay, Cameleon Harbour, in 1921.

August acquired a floathouse from a site on the mainland between Phillips and Frederick Arms and moved it across to East Thurlow Island, somewhere around Shoal Bay and Nodales Channel. The complex of sheds was winched up to a roughly logged area just above the high-tide line, and the young family lived there for about two years. August or Zaida took a photo from the house of tugs yarding a boom across the entrance to Phillips Arm.

Pearl identified another photo that showed the buildings making up the house, along with two more structures and an outhouse, all on floats and tied to a pier that, given its length, must be the one at Shoal Bay. That community, laid out on East Thurlow Island in 1895 after a gold find, once boasted three hotels and bars. August's old negative has printed up such deep space I

Right: Pearl and Leo, c. 1937.
August Schnarr photo. Image MCR 2006-8 courtesy of the Museum at Campbell River

Far right: Zaida, August, Pearl and Pansy Schnarr.
Schnarr family photo. Image MCR 8492 courtesy of the Museum at Campbell River

The Schnarr floathouse near Nodales Channel.
August Schnarr photo. Image MCR 11640 courtesy of the Museum at Campbell River

Left: Lansall pole cabin, Cameleon Harbour, Thurston Bay, Sonora Island.
Schnarr family photo. Image MCR 14392 courtesy of the Museum at Campbell River

Below: Log tow, entrance to Phillips Arm.
August Schnarr photo. Image MCR 20447-5 courtesy of the Museum at Campbell River

The Schnarr float camp at Shoal Bay. *August Schnarr photo. Image MCR 20447-20 courtesy of the Museum at Campbell River*

can count the pieces of laundry on the line and pick my way back, as I did when I visited the bay in 1990, to abandoned boxes of mining cores at the mouth of the road into that draw. Pearl said August laughed about what fools he thought men were, staking their lives on finding gold there.

The hand-hewn 30-foot-long, 5-foot-wide dugout sitting on the fore-edge of the float would become August's propeller-driven airboat.

"That white cruiser's our first boat, called *Hope*," Pearl said. "Don't know why, maybe because of the children. Sometimes we called it *Hopeless*, and later we called our boat *Loggerette*. Well, if there were loggers, we were loggerettes."

Even though the outfit looks ready to move, smoke rises from the floathouse chimneys and the sea looks a bit choppy. Maybe it was not a day to tow anything anywhere, or they may have been waiting, as they must if moving south to Bute, for a slack tide needed to traverse the rapids. Sometime around 1924/25 August did hitch the floats to a tug that towed them down Cordero Channel, through the Dent and Yuculta Rapids at Stuart Island and into the opaque, jade waters of Bute.

"That house was moving all the time," Pearl said. "For a while we were north of Fawn Bluff in lower Bute. Oh!" She and Glen laugh. "There were stories about a cave there. The Leask brothers put all their stuff inside. A rock slide closed it up."

Was this a backcountry treasure myth? The three Leask brothers were real enough to be photo-

The Schnarr floathouses, the gasboat *Hope* and the longboat at Fawn Bluff, Bute Inlet.
August Schnarr photo. Image MCR 20447-9 courtesy of the Museum at Campbell River

Below left: Leask Homestead, Fawn Bluff, painted by Charles Leask.
Easthope Brothers collection

Below: The Leask brothers, c.1920s.
Photographer unknown

graphed in the 1920s, and brother Charles painted their large homestead and waterpower shed in the bay at the mouth of Leask Lake, immediately south of Fawn Bluff at the entrance to Bute Inlet, opposite the mouth of Arran Rapids. When the Schnarrs anchored on the north side of Fawn Bluff, they would have met the three elderly Scots out and about in their 45-foot launch.

The country from Church House to Stuart Island, past Fawn Bluff and up Bute Inlet and river valley complex to an interface with the Tŝilhqot'in territory in the Chilcotin Plateau constituted the Homalco People's ancestral land. With the Klahoose and Sliammon Peoples, the

The Leask brothers, Henry Graham (born in 1851), Charles Hardy (1862) and Alfred (1863), were born in the Orkney Islands. Henry had been a sea captain, Alfred a banker and Charles an accountant. Intrigued by the Pacific Coast, the brothers moved to the mouth of Bute Inlet from New Zealand around 1913, during August Schnarr's first series of inlet explorations with his own brothers. Over sixteen years the well-educated Leasks, with more funds than most locals, built stone walls, walkways and a net shed with a set of boat ways, and laid water pipes from the lake to run a Pelton wheel, a small sawmill and a kiln so they could melt and pour a glass lens they were grinding for a telescope. Vegetarians, they tended a large garden and orchard. The Leasks' modest home was lined with bookshelves containing complete sets of Ruskin and Shakespeare. They became friends of the Easthope family, famous for their engines, and Easthope Brothers purchased Charles's painted panorama of the CPR steamships entering Burrard Inlet, and two more paintings looking into Bute Inlet and across the Strait of Georgia. Charles died at Fawn Bluff in early 1930. In the winter of 1933/34 both Alfred and Henry broke their legs. The brothers were taken home to Scotland.

Homalco are the most northerly grouping of Salish-language speakers. Current Homalco Chief Darren Blaney's recognition of the collapsed cave story and its relation to his family's claim to ownership in that area raises a question: Why were road builders, loggers and homesteaders like the Leasks and Schnarrs encouraged by the government to move right into Homalco village sites at the Orford, Homathko and Southgate Rivers and onto other locations they'd occupied for millennia? Bulletin #7, a 1924 Province of British Columbia Department of Lands publication, advertises land available for settlement from Toba Inlet, the home of the Klahoose People, to Queen Charlotte Sound. It promises arable land, mineral deposits and post offices at Bruce's Landing on Stuart Island at the mouth of Bute and farther up-inlet in Orford Bay. Another post office, a store and a steamer service are said to be available at the modern Homalco settlement of Church House, south of Fawn Bluff. Otherwise, the Indigenous people living throughout the entire area are not mentioned.

Pearl said the Schnarrs' Fawn Bay float camp was moved up the inlet after it was blown out by a big wind, and they squatted in upper Bute from 1925 until August obtained a twenty-year lease on April 11, 1928. Situated at A17, Range 1, Coast District, it contained 17 acres: "Commencing at the most southerly Southwest corner of Lot 556, Range 1, Coast District, being a point on high water mark of Bute Inlet: thence east 20 chains more or less along the south boundary of said Lot 556 to the south corner thereof; thence south 10 chains; thence 15 chains more or less to high water mark; thence north-westerly along said high water mark to the point of commencement." That site, south of Purcell Point on the east shore of Bute Inlet, came to be known locally as Schnarr's Bay or Landing. The floating complex seen in photos taken at Shoal Bay and Fawn Bluff was hauled ashore there, with the outhouse out over water as was common. August's plan was to handlog in summer and trap in fall while clearing land and building a garden and orchard. Once the family was established in Bute, Pearl said, he spent weeks alone exploring and trapping the Homathko Valley or up at Chilko Lake in cabins and lean-tos he'd built.

August Schnarr Bute Inlet B.C. 1928 | 2

Miscellany

Date	Items	Spent ~~Charges~~	Received ~~Credits~~	Balance
~~Jan. 1.~~	~~Carrolls E. S. Co. Van. Radio repair~~	~~1.50~~		~~1.50~~
~~Jan. 31.~~	~~B. Brines Thurlow. Boarding child~~	~~15.00~~		~~15.00~~
~~Jan. 31.~~	~~E. Adkins Heriot Bay.~~	~~165.75~~		~~165.75~~
~~Jan. 31~~	~~Storekeeper Stuart Island. Gasoline~~	~~10.80~~		~~10.80~~
Feb. 18.	Affidavit on Cougar Bounty	2.50	~~2.50~~	
Feb. 20.	Hudsons Bay Co. Furs sold.	~~150.00~~	150.00	
Mar. 10.	Freight on Cougar skins	1.20		
Mar. 16.	Cheque for Cougar bounty		160.00	
Mar. 17.	{Powell River Canvas}	20.00		
Mar. 24	{Above received}			
April. 14.	C. Thompson– Thurlow. Mdse.	10.20		
April 30.	Hudsons Bay Co.. Furs Sold.		62.00	
May 5.	Hudsons Bay Co. Furs Sold.		30.00	
May. –	Cougar Skins Sold.		15.00	
May. 14.	Wages paid in Full. A. Holm.	27.00		
June 2.	(1927) Compensation + Medical Aid	15.00		
Aug. 4	Stamp Hammer 34A	2.00		
Aug. 27.	Wages paid in full A. Holm	170.15		
Aug. 31.	" " " " H. Tallgard	372.16		
Sept. 1.	Recieved From P. McDonald. Thurlow.	~~100.00~~	100.00	
Sept. 3	Paid C.C. Thompson in full	13.95		
Sep. 1	Mdse.	3.40		
Oct. 16.	Homalko Survey Party Trip		300.00	
Oct. 30.	" " " "		14.00	
Nov. 15	1 Live mink by A. Paul	10.00		

Top: The Schnarr house complex at Schnarr's Landing, c. 1927/28.

August Schnarr photo. Image MCR 20447-21 courtesy of the Museum at Campbell River

Left: A page from the Schnarr family record books, 1928.

Image MCR 79-1 courtesy of the Museum at Campbell River

Above: One of three Schnarr trapping cabins in the Homathko Valley.

August Schnarr photo. Image MCR 20447-22 courtesy of the Museum at Campbell River

Alfred Waddington's Gold Road, Homathko Camp to Mosley Creek

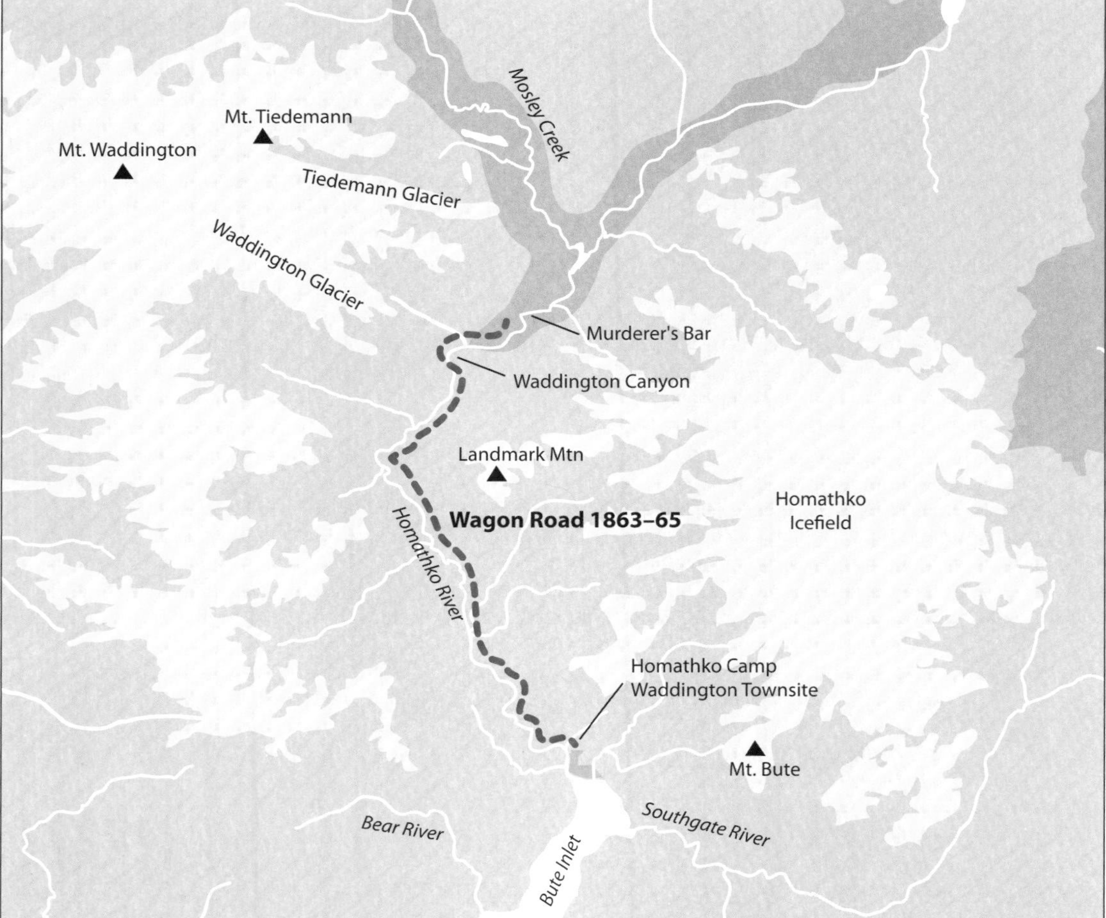

A neat hand recorded the family income and expenses for 1928 in one of a clutch of school notebooks the Schnarrs retained from their early years.[4] A number of furs were sold to the Hudson's Bay Company, a surprising $160 received as cougar bounty, $314 from a survey party August guided and $15 paid for boarding Pansy on Thurlow Island for school. The $2 paid for an official timber mark—"Stamp Hammer 34A"—indicates August had a handlogging sale, and he paid wages to A. Holm and H. Tallgard.

Both Glen and Pearl say that while trapping up the Homathko Valley, August searched for remains of the road Alfred Waddington tried to build in the early 1860s, and one of the cabins he built was near what came to be called "Murderer's Bar" in recognition of the road crew killings.

In the interviews about his life taped in 1977, August, precise about movement through the territory, said Waddington built a road from the Waddington townsite, at the head of Bute Inlet, along the Homathko River, "32 miles up, and bridges across all the creeks. And there's one or two bad creeks on the way up there, ones that clear the streams . . . [Waddington's road crew] had what they call a ferry crossing, almost at the [Homathko] canyon . . . Then above that there's a high bank of gravel, the river hitting against that. And you get up on this bank, there's a big bear trail of course, there's always a big bear trail along the river.

"Where the [Waddington] road leads up again towards the canyon . . . [It's] within a quarter of a mile of there, and there's a little creek comes in from the wood, from the river. Whenever I build a cabin I want water, and wood of course too. So I went right back in there against those mountains . . . about 400 feet . . . and built a cabin."[5]

When interviewed by Maud Emery for Victoria's *Colonist* newspaper in 1960, August laughed at those who told him he should never travel alone in such a landscape. "In that country, where mountains, canyons, valleys, lakes, rivers and river-jams hold traps for the unwary and inexperienced, if you make a mistake, it's your last. I never leave anything to chance. 'We might make it' is not good enough for me. A man is just as safe alone, perhaps safer. Suppose I broke my leg up there in that frozen mountainous region and I have a partner with me. Can he help me? No. He can't pack me out over that kind of terrain, and if he leaves me to go for help, I'd be frozen to death before he got back."[6]

However, August's trips were not always solitary. Pearl's album contained a photograph of Wardy MacDonald, storekeeper at Shoal Bay, and Teddy Hill, a forest ranger from Thurston Bay, sitting in the bow of August's longboat. The 30-foot dugout is bunted up to a gravel bar, likely in a Homathko back eddy. Looking at the next photo, Pearl said, "That's Dad's canoe with August and Teddy Hill making fun of people photographing their large fish." The camera case for August's Kodak 3, a portable of its day, sits on the boat bow. There are paddles and poles, and although that trip may be a story, his longboats, appearing over and over in August's photos, were a bigger story, an ongoing experiment allowing him to move himself and materials far upriver.

Wardy MacDonald, left, and Teddy Hill in the bow of August's longboat. *August Schnarr photo. Image MCR 14414 courtesy of the Museum at Campbell River*

This was not August's first dugout. In his photo notes he explained he'd seen Indigenous people carve long, flat canoes for travelling up the Klinaklini River in Knight Inlet. A cedar log dugout, the centre charred and hacked out, then steamed to flexibility and widened, as cedar can be with water heated by hot rocks, was ideal for navigating inlet rivers. The current in the Homathko is extremely swift, and poling or paddling any distance upstream was arduous for one man. An outboard engine required a propeller and rudder that took space below the waterline and caused strandings on the seasonally shifting sandbars. Sometime after these late 1920s photos, August carved an airplane-type propeller out of wood to be used with an inboard engine, transforming the dugout into an airboat. August's first propellers were too heavy, but the final set, now on Pearl's lawn, carved from the light, clear-grained cedar planks he used to make stretcher boards for curing animal skins, has the elegance of necessary form. Did he learn something of aerodynamics from his brother Johnny, who installed airplane engines in the high-speed boats he used to run booze into the United States during Prohibition?[7] Pearl said

Teddy Hill and August Schnarr, with August's dugout canoe, poling pole and camera case, upriver.
August Schnarr photo. Image MCR 14389 courtesy of the Museum at Campbell River

Zaida with Pansy, Pearl and baby Marion, Arran Rapids, c. 1926.
August Schnarr photo. Image MCR 8492 courtesy of the Museum at Campbell River

her father took a correspondence course in engineering around 1927; despite having had almost no schooling, August got 100 per cent on the course. "He would work and work on a problem, like building an electromagnet to pick up the heavy boom chains needed in his logging show."

The final airboat propeller was attached to an elaborately pieced wooden hub connected to steel bearings. Everything was bolted to a welded iron tripod that sat at the back of the boat. In early models, four narrow belts connected the propeller wheel to a Briggs and Stratton gas engine placed inside the boat below the pedestal. A lever at the stern of the boat raised and lowered the rudder in shallow water. When a metal cage surrounded the prop, the ensemble resembled a skookum North Woods cousin to a Florida Swamp airboat. August carried loads of lumber and tools up the Homathko to build trapping cabins, and with the airboat he could transport material up the inlet at 10 miles per hour.[8]

Pearl turned to a new album page. "That's Zaida," she said, "sitting on a rock with Pansy, me, and Marion, born in 1926, in her arms." In the photo, the Arran Rapids, west of the mouth of Bute, can be seen ebbing north between the mainland and Stuart Island.

Eighty years later, Pearl bent down into the next image's sepia-toned room. It's the only photo, museum archivists say, of an old floathouse interior, and a nice one at that. A crib, high chair, table and two kitchen chairs hover in light drifting through sunshine-filled curtains. The head of a two-point buck is mounted on a water-stained wall. Below, to the right of the crib is, . . . "a box," Pearl said, "used for Marion to sleep in when she came along. I slept in the crib. The box slid under in the day."

Did life with laughing Zaida prompt August's domestic photos, or is this sole interior image Zaida's eye and her photographic voice? The album contains images of the girls in a tub on the

Top left: Interior of Schnarr floathouse. *August or Zaida Schnarr photo. Image MCR 11639 courtesy of the Museum at Campbell River*

Top right: Pearl, Pansy and Marion in a tub on the floathouse deck, Bute Inlet, August 19, 1925. *August or Zaida Schnarr photo. Image MCR 14411 courtesy of the Museum at Campbell River*

house float, with rabbit and marten cages, or standing next to a dead cougar. Pearl said Zaida made the children rabbit-skin clothes and canned the rabbit meat no one would buy. "We ate it for years!"

"Did you like it?" I asked.

"We didn't know any different."

"We don't really know very much about our mother," Pearl said. "We were sent off to school and she and Dad stayed in Bute. We never saw them. When my mother died of cancer in 1932 and Dad was left with three girls, he decided to move to Owen Bay. He brought the house down inlet, towing it with a little old Easthope engine he had. Coming down, about at Stuart Island, a wind came up. He couldn't do anything about it. It just broke up the float and the house went down to the bottom. Lost everything. At Owen Bay he found some sheds, took them apart and made a house. We'd been alone a lot in Bute, and now we had the Schiblers next door, but we girls still spent summers alone in Bute while Dad went fishing. As he got older, Dad's desire to be in Bute became absolute, and when I was thirteen he moved us all back up Bute permanently."

"Why did he do that?"

"To avoid pregnancies."

That was one of Pearl's conversation stoppers.

"The Landing had a nice gravel beach, rare in Bute," she continued. "It faced directly south and the big joke was that across channel was the Paradise Valley. Dad said it was one of the worst places he'd been. Buggy! There were Indians living further up-inlet at Cumsack Creek then, in those sorts of houses they built, not much. They never seemed to build a real house. At Orford Bay I saw those hieroglyphics they made up on the bluff next to the river mouth. Way up on the cliff.

"We always had nice trim houses, always a full woodshed, that was the kind of man he was. Big garden. Grew raspberries and loganberries. Canned everything. We also had a root shed, double-layered walls filled with sawdust to keep stuff all winter. Made jam and the Indians traded fish and baskets for jam."

She pulled clippings out of a folder to add to those pasted in the album. The girls became known in a larger world after Quadra Island writer Francis Dickie published the article "Cougar Pets" in 1936.

"Oh, we were in different papers, *Maclean's*, all kinds of write-ups. It didn't mean much to us kids. They were just cats. Now we wish we'd taken more pictures."

Marion titled a *Cougar Companions* album photo of Pearl holding the cougar Girlie "Happiness is . . ." I was so startled by the image I wasn't sure I could read their emotions properly. Is the cougar purring, as she said they did, that they loved being petted and stroked? Is the mutual affection big news? Pearl, looking closely at the photo with me, was eye to eye with herself eye to eye with the cat, her arm lightly around it, holding Girlie up to her, left hand soft on soft fur. Pearl's face pressed to the cat's could be her son Glen's, could be Zaida's, so alike do they look.

How would you like a mountain lion for a playmate?

By FRANCIS DICKIE

Cougar Pets

"Nice kitty!" "Bur-r-r," replied Leo.

ON THE lonely wilderness island of Sonora, off the coast of British Columbia, three girls—Marion, Pearl and Pansy Schnarr—have brought up from babyhood two unique pets.

In January, 1935, their father, August Schnarr, a noted trapper, killed a large female mountain lion or cougar. As he was skinning it he noticed that the animal had recently become a mother. There is a bounty of $20 per head on these destructive animals, which will kill anything from a cat to a cow, so he backtracked through the snow and finally located the den at the foot of a fallen cedar tree. There he found four blind, mewing kittens. He threw them into his packsack and carried them to his cabin.

His three daughters—Marion aged eleven, Pearl twelve, and Pansy fourteen—had been motherless since infancy, and their hearts went out to the helpless kittens. They fed them warm canned milk out of a pop bottle with a baby's nipple fastened on top, and at the end of fourteen days the kittens opened their eyes.

Two of the kittens died, but when summer come, the two surviving mountain lions (which also are known as pumas, cougars, panthers and "painters"), now grown to the size of small dogs, roamed about the yard and even ventured into the forest. But always they returned.

For some eight months this idyllic state of happy kittenhood continued, then one afternoon Marion saw Leo, the larger of the two lions, sneaking toward the corral in which was kept one of the family pigs. Running at full speed, she reached the corral just as Leo did. She sprang between the pig and mountain lion, slapped the latter across the face, seized him by the collar and dragged him away.

Pens were now built for the animals and they were chained to them, but one day Leo broke free and chased a neighbor's goat. Pansy ran after her pet and seized his chain, and the animal became docile in her hands. Later, Leo escaped again and roamed the woods all night, only to return to his friends in the morning.

For two years now, the Schnarr girls have kept the two mountain lions as pets, playing with them as other girls play with house cats, often with an empty tomato can which is used as a sort of football. Yet no stranger dares approach the animals. Occasionally the girls doctor their pets, the latter submitting to treatment with even more docility than the average house cat.

Thus on a lonely island three girls and two ordinarily savage beasts have grown to maturity together—a unique companionship, perhaps the first on record on the North American Continent.

Marion, Pansy and Pearl Schnarr with their pet cougars.

Girlie.

Pansy, Pearl and Marion with Girlie and Leo. Trying to get both cougars in one picture sometimes met with resistance.

Above: *Cougar Companions* album page.
Image MCR 2006-8 courtesy of the Museum at Campbell River

Left: Pearl Schnarr and Girlie.
Pearl Schnarr album. Unknown commercial photographer. Image MCR 15626 courtesy of the Museum at Campbell River

Pearl may have been showing off a bit for the photographer, and why not? She looks confident and the cat is sure about Pearl. August said the girls could do anything with them; they'd just snarl at him. In another photo you see the two cougars, each attached to enormous stumps. The chains were needed at Owen Bay to protect the neighbour's livestock and to keep the cats from following the girls to school. They were careful not to let them kill anything, not to give them raw meat. They fed them fish and oatmeal.

Two alder leaves at the left foreground of the photo establish distance between cougar and photographer. That's where I am, a careful distance away on the surface of the print, but I'm dying to be there, holding that cat at Owen Bay. Or are they up Bute? They took the cougars everywhere with them on boats, let them roam free while underway. Girlie once fell overboard and had to swim until they came back to get her. Where the photo was taken depends on how old Pearl is.

"I stayed at home in Bute until I couldn't stand it," she said. "Not one more fight with him. I said, 'I'm a chip off the old block.' Mad. Left at fifteen, went to Vancouver, married a military

Jack McPhee and Ed Adkin with a dead wolf.
August Schnarr photo. Image MCR 6697 courtesy of the Museum at Campbell River

man, moved to Winnipeg. Pansy married Lloyd Fair to get away. Married at Redonda Bay on the *Columbia*. Aunt Flossie came."

Remembering, she was angry again.

I turn back to an earlier album photo, a black shape dangling by a cruelly broken leg from a tripod, a haunting foil to Pearl and Girlie's affectionate embrace.

"August said he could call a wolf," said Pearl, suddenly proud of his skills. "It would come, could be shot. Fur was money, $2.50 for any pelt. You could buy a sack of flour with that. For wolves you got $150.00!"

Wolves eat deer, people eat bread and deer. No one eats wolf. Wolves you wear. Low sun casts an arced shadow of that wolf, the tripod and two men who aren't alike. On the left, an upcoast dude—"Jack," Pearl said, "that rascal Jack McPhee"—hat in hand, sticks a knife in a tripod leg. August said, "McPhee pretended to be almost anything and wasn't anything, claimed to be a trapper but he was just a nuisance."

"Lots of people don't know some wolves were black like that," Pearl said. "The other man is Ed Adkin who ran a logging camp at Eva Creek, as the Teaquahan was then called."

Small and compact, laced into white rubber boots, a roll-yer-own hanging from his lower lip, Ed stands straight, gun upright, facing forward as if on parade, hamming it up. The abrupt rise behind them makes me think the men are up the Homathko River, perhaps in 1928, when Ed was witness for the Schnarr lease.

Looking at a photo of Ed with a cougar, his son and a girl, Pearl said, "That child is me," rather firmly, as if there were some dispute. In a second related photo including August, Pansy appears about five, so it could be 1926.

Ed Adkin's son, whom Pearl called "Brother," with August, a dead cougar and Pansy, Bute Inlet, c. 1926. *August Schnarr negatives. Image MCR 14424 courtesy of the Museum at Campbell River*

When Pearl tired, Glen took me out to the big shed to show me August's extra propellers, herring rake and pelt-stretching boards that all retain a fine, dark brown surface attributable to a coating of the Bute wax that is unique to the inlet. This naturally produced substance, appearing on the surface of the inlet water only in conditions of extreme wind and cold, was used as an all-round grease and preservative. "Dad would completely fill that canoe with those Bute wax balls appearing in Bear Bay in bad weather," Pearl had said. Glen dug a soft, buttery sample from a barrel August had moved to Heriot Bay and slid it into a jar.

Late in life, on Quadra, August used Bute wax to grease the rails for hauling his last long-

boat, which he often drove without the propeller's protective cage. He once came into the dock at Hill Island full speed, removed the brightwork off the side of a yacht with this rotor and walked away without a word. He hewed a dugout bathtub at Heriot Bay to keep his carving hand in. "I burned it," Pansy's son Norm Fair told me, "cleaning up after he died. Then I thought, I should have kept that wooden tub!"

The longboat became smothered in blackberry bushes after his death, but the propeller sitting on the Macklins' lawn still turned smoothly in its pieced wooden shaft.

It was late when I got back to Cortes Island after visiting the Macklins that day, and Glen's buttery Bute wax sample had melted into amber oil. Pearl died three months later.

Glen Macklin with Bute wax.
Judith Williams photo

Pearl remembered the longboat as a container for the mysterious Bute wax balls. Her rich explication of the album images led me to assemble a different kind of container: a Bute dossier based on prints from the Campbell River Museum's Schnarr negative files and copies of household ephemera donated by the family. I found more of August's photos in "The 1928–1930 Water Power Investigation of the Taseko–Chilcotin–Homathko," a report prepared for BC's Water Rights Branch. F.W. Knewstubb, the province's chief hydraulic engineer, set out the findings of the survey group August Schnarr guided up the river valleys.

I began to position images in time and place, interleaving Marion's *Cougar Companions* album stories about life with the cougars, her dates and locations, with the water report and Pansy's 1938/39 diary from the Schnarr fonds.[9] Then, using prints of August's photos as playing cards, I laid out images in suits in a skewed variant of the game Patience. I wanted to formulate a Schnarr photo taxonomy based on date, sequence, subject, archival documentation and August's tools and inventions. As I boated through the area again, I was able to anchor the Schnarrs' peripatetic floathouse camp at Shoal Bay, Fawn Bluff or deep in Bute Inlet and connect images to material related to the trapping, logging and gardening that sustained the Schnarrs through the Depression and into the 1960s.

The photograph collection begged to be examined as a social record of the remote location and the role of the three girls in their economic system, but I also developed an appreciation of the photos as conceptually and aesthetically intriguing images. I wondered to what degree August had consciously staged his photos, and from what point of view? The striking photographs of cougars hugged, treed by dogs or skinned could not help but lead me to an uneasy consideration of our complex relationship to animals we kill, wear and/or eat and those we do not. August's agenda was different.

Pearl had stressed that the media images of the girls and cougars presented the girls' life differently from how they experienced it. Journalists unnecessarily romanticized and softened a story that, given the grinding, hard-logging way August and the girls lived, planting potatoes, canning fish, making jam, building boats, booming logs, hauling 100-pound boom chains and raising cougars, all in water-access-only isolation, was already remarkable. "They even got the cats' names wrong," Pearl said, "and called me Daisy," imprecisions irritating to August's competent and necessarily pragmatic daughters.

In the process of laying out image suits, I found that the subject of one photograph might extend sideways, connect to another image and open a new track; memory might stage a small drama, usher in a new character or send me on a historical or theoretical sidetrack. Some stories are just too good not to follow. The dossier shook free of the *Cougar Companions* albums, and with the voices of remaining family members and their inlet neighbours adding commentary, I assembled a broader version of the Schnarrs' lives in Bute's exhilarating, taxing and isolated environment. It takes note of how the girls and our views of them were and are affected by their unique circumstances, by their own staging and making of images, and by being photographed by Zaida, August and outsiders. In the memory theatre, photographs can replace actual events for the Schnarrs, their descendants or me.

INTERLUDE I

THE KODAK WITNESS

AT FIRST PHOTOGRAPHIC IMPLEMENTS WERE RELATED TO TECHNIQUES OF CABINETMAKING AND THE MACHINERY OF PRECISION: CAMERAS, IN SHORT, WERE CLOCKS FOR SEEING.

—ROLAND BARTHES,

CAMERA LUCIDA: REFLECTIONS ON PHOTOGRAPHY

June 10, 2011

The pickup skidded to a halt in the yard and Glen Macklin held two objects out the window. "Want these? In a hurry, but I dropped by Dad's and picked them up."

One was the camera Pearl had saved. "Oh yes!"

He got out, handed me a small wooden stand holding a horseshoe, propped a brown leather case on his knee and slid out the camera.

"It's August's. There's a picture of it in the canoe up the river. He took it with him. It says 1910 somewhere, I think. This is how you open it."

He clicked slick little levers and slid the bellows out. The interior was immaculate. I wanted to take a picture of Glen opening the camera with the camera August had carried up in the wilderness to picture his world and add that to Pearl's *Cougar Companions*.

August Schnarr's Kodak #3 camera and case.
Judith Williams photo

"I've seen a great photo taken upriver at the Homathko Canyon by August," I said. "Because it shows the problem Waddington faced trying to put the road through to the Interior, it's reproduced everywhere. This must be the camera that took that and most of the album photos. Where would he have gotten film developed?"

"Don't know. Brought you this mule shoe. It's from the 1860s. Carl Larson found it way up on Waddington's road works and made the stand with wood from one of August's trapping cabins he found. Larson walked into the Interior following Waddington's proposed road and the old grease trail, walked in on the Mosley Creek route, the right way to go, he says. Found the mule shoe and gave it to me. I tried to fit the propeller at Dad's into the truck today but I couldn't get it in."

After Glen left, I worried about that propeller. He had loaned me August's pelt-stretching boards and pole and steel spikes from the Southgate rail line

Above: Mule shoe and stand.
Judith Williams photo

Left: The formidable currents in the Homathko River canyon forced Waddington's 1860s road crew to climb up and over the cliffs and construct a cantilevered road south along a sheer wall from the north end.
August Schnarr photo. Image MCR 14405 courtesy of the Museum at Campbell River

for my Bute Inlet museum installation. He knew the wooden propeller should be saved, but the steel stand was a wide-stanced, awkward thing.

I turned over the abutted pieces of wood. The dainty shoe was hung on a brass tack set on the upright piece above an engraved plaque: "Waddington's Wagon Road, 1862–1864. Found Sept. 7, 1992."

History in the hand.

People say August was the only person to master Bute Inlet's fierce winds and boat far up the seasonally shifting rivers. He was hired to rescue others who tried. The hand-hewn, propeller-driven airboat illustrates his compulsion to work and work at something until he'd solved the problem. The camera, a circa 1910 Kodak #3, using a twelve-image roll of film, is another tool, a clock to tell us his time. Where and when he bought it is unknown. Photographer Henry Twiddle operated a store, post office and hotel from 1911 until the early 1950s at Granite Bay on the west side of Quadra Island. It was accessible south from Nodales Channel and west from the Schnarrs' 1930s home in Owen Bay, on Sonora Island, via Okisollo and Discovery Channels. Pioneer coastal photographer Francis Barrow bought a Thornton-Pickard cine camera from Twiddle in 1936 to shoot movies during his yearly upcoast cruises. Did Twiddle stock film?

August Schnarr's Kodak #3 camera.
Judith Williams photo

A "David Spencer" negatives envelope in the Schnarr fonds provides one clue to the source of August's camera. Spencer opened his Hastings Street store in Vancouver in 1907, the year August first arrived in British Columbia. Its photography department sold cameras and film, and offered developing. It became Eaton's in 1948. A "Woodward's" photo envelope indicates some developed film came from Woodward's Store, also on Hastings, which did a lively mail-order business of foodstuffs and general merchandise that arrived upcoast on the Union Steamship from Vancouver. When the ship docked at Surge Narrows, Stuart Island or Church House, locals like the Schnarrs boated in from all over the area for mail, groceries, gas and social interaction. The family fonds contain a number of Woodward's order books and waybills.

2

READING IMAGES

What do I mean when I say I am "reading" the Schnarr images? If I lay the photographs down in suits, adding August's late-life commentary, Pearl's explications and Pansy's and Marion's notes, I create a shaky timeline. What can I learn? Person, place, perhaps a date? If I really look, I might discern a tonal or psychological ambiance, a reason for the photo, perhaps a larger meaning. Here is young Marion around 1928–30, with a caged mink, a note says. Or is that a marten? How about those striking diagonals and dreamy layers of sun-filtering mesh? How does Marion, or how do I, feel about caged animals raised for fur? An image like this, suggesting a more complex depth to an early Bute family photo sequence, can send me off on a new image run. Conflicting stories can send me running in circles. Memory is not a science. A "reading" is not necessarily conventional history.

Marion with mink or marten at Schnarr's Landing animal sheds.
August Schnarr photo. Image MCR 11641 courtesy of the Museum at Campbell River

The oldest dated image in Pearl's *Cougar Companions* is said to show August at the "Grizzly" on the Klinaklini Glacier (see photo on page x). In the interview he gave the Campbell River Museum in 1977, August said he'd trekked there in 1913, which was when the photo was taken with his camera. It was *not* taken when he was guiding surveyors for the BC government's Water Rights Branch up the Homathko and Southgate Rivers. However, the same photo is in the BC government's "Water Power Investigation" report labelled "Foot of Tiedemann Glacier, Homathko River." On the same page of the report is a Schnarr photo that *could be* the Tiedemann Glacier, and these two images illustrate the caution needed when dating August's work based on his, Marion's or Pearl's later memories and the notes of others. The negative of August looking back at us looking at him and the glacier formation is in the museum's Schnarr collection, donated by his family, and as important to me as the location is seeing the case for the camera he used from 1910 into the '60s strapped to his suspenders. A companion shot *is* firmly labelled "Schnarr standing on the Kleena Kleen Glacier."[10]

August told his interviewers he was last in Knight Inlet in 1915/16, and while there he learned to carve and pole the long, shallow dugouts the Tenaktak People used on the Franklin and Klinaklini Rivers. In their earliest coastal days, when logging ended in the fall, August and his brothers, who had joined him in British Columbia, took themselves as far into the wilderness as they could to hunt and trap. I had asked Pearl where August learned his woodcraft.

"They lived down in Centralia, Washington," she said. "German Americans. August was eldest. When Dad and Johnny and Gus got older, they chased their father away with his own gun. Drank. They farmed and hunted for a living. Marion wrote *Rumrunner* about Johnny's

Ray Walker with grizzlies shot by August, Knight Inlet, c. 1915/16. *August Schnarr photo. Image MCR 20447-42 courtesy of the Museum at Campbell River*

activities out of Victoria during the US alcohol Prohibition from 1920 to 1933. He visited Bute sometimes. Smart aleck! They didn't get along."

Like any person wishing to survive in the backcountry, August was precise about location and distance. While in Knight Inlet he told interviewers Skogan and Havelaar that he "caught the Klinaklini River there clean through the canyon to the Interior. At the head of Knights there used to be an Indian reserve, great big totem poles. I used to take the canoes upriver, and that's where I learnt how to . . . make canoes and handle them. I used to take them up the canyon to that big glacier. I had a shack there right at the canyon mouth. There's a creek comes in from the Klinaklini Glacier, over all the way down to the gravel bar. Then it comes onto the river and just there, there's a canyon. Well, just above that, in there, I had a shack."

August and his interviewers were usually looking at his photos to spark such memories, as Pearl and I did going through *Cougar Companions.*

"There's Ray Walker [with] three grizzlies I shot up in Knight," August said. "Shot at the old one but she ran off."

Pearl said August partnered with Ray Walker, and the men trapped together in Knight during 1915/16. The photo of Ray with three grizzlies may be August's first image promoting his hunting skills. He was convinced he could earn a living in one of the inlets.

When August returned from trapping in Knight in 1916, he logged around Port Hardy on Vancouver Island, and in Shoal and Rock Bays. He was handlogging in Blind Channel, between West and East Thurlow Islands, when the larger world intruded and he and Johnny, who had moved back south, were drafted into different outfits to fight in the Great War.

"Year of '16? '17?" August said. "I went overseas in the First World War. I was in the American Army . . . I wasn't a [Canadian] citizen yet. They drafted me from this side. I coulda been back in the woods here and I wouldn't have known . . . but I went over and . . . it was quite an experience all right. I shoulda died there. Like they said, 'It's hell on you boys'! Most of them died with

Homesteaders on the Southgate.
Image B-05985 courtesy of the Royal BC Museum and Archives

In the 1960s, Ray Walker's younger brother, Dennis, related how their family and other settlers took up land at the Southgate River Township in Bute in the 1890s.[11] Homesteaders claimed sites at the Homalco village Miimaya (*MEE-a-Mian*), an important Homalco fishing area, where two types of tidal traps were used. Previously, when intertribal warfare ended, Interior Tŝilhqot'in People camped there in fall with the Homalco to smoke-dry fish for winter storage.[12]

Dennis's father, W.G. Walker, was living in England in 1892 when he heard of a proposed Grand Trunk Pacific (now the CNR) railway route from Chilcotin territory to the head of Bute Inlet. He brought his wife and eight children to Vancouver. Then, Dennis said, "Father left for the upcoast to 'land hunt' in a sailboat with two men who were going prospecting. They put him off at the head of Bute Inlet where three trappers, Ben Franklin, Tony Bernhardt and Mart Blanchfield, lived."

Franklin, a pioneer trailblazer and old-time trapper, owned a ranch at Tatla Lake in Chilcotin country. It is said he and his wife came from the Chilcotin over a well-used but dangerous Indigenous trail to take up Bute land.

Dennis's father liked the Southgate and moved his family there in March 1893. They stayed with the three trappers, who built them a log house where a shallow flat of land swings west of the river mouth. Mr. Walker bought 40 acres upriver from Ben Franklin.

"As soon as we were settled in," Dennis said, "we had to start clearing land. How we managed is beyond me, for we knew nothing about backwoods life, but we got by."

On June 25, 1895, the *Vancouver News-Advertiser* claimed settlers were coming "in fairly large numbers." The reporter noted that the local merchant had paid out $5,000 for the best bear skins he had ever seen, and "now that bear season was over, he had several of the Indians logging for him. They appear respectable, well dressed, have plenty of money and are erecting some good houses. Their gardens are also looking well."

With the help of Homalco People they employed, the Southgate settlers raised potatoes, but the spuds shipped to Vancouver barely paid for their freight. A newborn Walker baby died, and then two of their daughters; the railway took another route; and the family, like the rest of the settlers, moved on.

pneumonia and dysentery. There's nothing to eat, laying on the cold ground . . . you see, when you read about things like that, you never get the truth. You always hear about battles they're fighting and how they get their wounded out. The wounded are left lying there! I got pneumonia, just got sicker and sicker . . . they picked me up . . . took me back behind the hill . . . behind the shelling, but the shells came right over the top . . . killed thirteen. Well, the next morning I was half covered with dirt."

Invalided out to a hospital, August eventually made it back to the Shoal Bay area.

"When I was drafted I had a 30-foot canoe and trapping stuff I left with George Bruce to sell for me while I was away. When I got back he had nothing. I said, 'When I get you one day we'll settle this.' If I want to fight, I must be in the right. Then I am determined to carry it through. [Holds up fist.] It never failed me. I wouldn't back down for anyone.

Hastings logging crew, Rock Bay. August is at front right.
Image MCR 6696 courtesy of the Museum at Campbell River

"I saw him one day in Shoal Bay. I was working in a mill. He came out of a store wearing a big overcoat, had his hands in his pockets. [I said,] 'Now I've got you. Now—Mr. Bruce, here it is.' He tried to push by me. 'Get on your guard,' I said, and he pushed by and I landed one right on him. Down he went! Three times I knocked him down. A bunch came over. He said, 'This man hit me without a warning.' They all got in a boat. I got in the boat. I said, 'Every time I see you I'm gonna hit you.'

"Well, there was one thing and another. I got married. [When] I saw him again he was working in a hardware store as a bookkeeper. Mr. Bruce . . . [when he] saw me, he was gone."

August must have carved another dugout, the one Pearl identified in the 1920s Shoal Bay photo as his "30-foot canoe." Now, with a wife and two children, August struggled to make his float camp and boats help him work for himself. "I trapped in the winter and handlogged in the summer." To facilitate his economic plan, August wanted trapping cabins or shelters every 10 miles up the Homathko Valley, where the winter furs were best, and a homestead nearby.

In a photo Pearl let me copy, two handmade paddles lean against a raft pulled up on a snowy bank out of an opaque stretch of water. An axe is stuck in the raft, and a gun leans against a rucksack at an angle I can't recommend. Behind the canvas rucksack is a beautiful young man. Fingering the torn edge of the photo, Pearl said, "That's Rankin Robertson from Cortes."

"Rankin Robertson? A kind of lady-killer," Marion said on the phone in 2010—remembered that, even though she insisted she remembered nothing.

I want to climb right into that sepia scene and join Rankin as he bends a little forward, ready to go. According to Robertson family lore, when he was sixteen, in the fall of 1920, Rankin went up Bute from Cortes Island to stay with August and help look for trapping cabin locations. When he didn't return, his family feared he'd died, but his mother noted in her diary that he strolled in for his June birthday.[13]

Rankin Robertson, Homathko Valley, 1920.
August Schnarr photo. Image MCR 20,447-31 courtesy of the Museum at Campbell River

The big rucksack on the raft in the photo would be heavy even empty. August was fussy about his gear; everything he floated and hiked up the valleys had to work. "Good enough is not good enough," he said. There was no room for mistakes. Grandson Norm Fair described how August sometimes used round barrels, covered in waterproof canvas, to which were attached two bucksaw blades that curved forward over the shoulders, to carry gear up the valleys. He wanted dry food and supplies. Firewood was essential.

Where *is* Rankin? He and August are going to, or have come from, somewhere that necessitated a raft. Contemporary Homathko Valley explorer Carl Larson said August crossed smaller high tarns like Law wa Lake between the West and East Forks of the Homathko by falling 10-inch trees and rafting them together with cross-braces. To cross rivers he entered the river so it swept the raft downstream but to the opposite side.

Elmer Ellingson, son of the inventor of the Ellingson jack that August used when handlogging, said Rankin told him, "August Schnarr and I were travelling on foot up the Homathko River where August had a trapline, and we travelled relatively easily on one side of the river, until we reached the steep walls of a canyon. At this point August said the trail was much easier on the far side of the river, and he proposed we cross the canyon. He took his axe out of his pack and chopped down a tall Douglas fir to fall across the canyon to form a temporary bridge high above the wild water below. August then donned his pack, climbed up on the trunk of the fir with his axe in one hand and walked steadily across the bridge, knocking a few limbs off the tree trunk as he went."

Elmer said, "Rankin, watching this display of confidence and balance as Schnarr crossed the canyon, felt less confident and put his pack on the 'bridge' ahead of himself and 'cooned' it across the log on all fours."

Elmer's son Andy added, "This description by Rankin Robertson was very impressive as we knew him to be a very capable woodsman himself, not easily backing down from a challenge. He was clearly impressed with Schnarr's ability and self-confidence."[14]

Rankin Robertson, August Schnarr and Charlie Rasmussen, upriver.
Pearl Schnarr album

Pearl identified men in another album photo, suggesting an adventure in a warmer season: "That's Rankin, Dad and Charlie on the right." Surrounded by frypan, billy-can of milk, plates and utensils, they sit on a gravel bar on some thread of the mercurial Homathko River, which will likely blast that bar and its tangle of stumps into another position in next July's melt. We get a good look at four boot soles. Pearl's "Charlie" is identified by Rita Rasmussen as *her* father, Charlie. He has one foot in the air and rolls toward his right arm, which is obscured by a serpentine branch. August crouches, one knee on the ground, his right hand casting strong finger shadows behind the head of Rankin, who lounges like a sharply foreshortened odalisque, lush lipped, looking straight at the camera, handsome as a star.

If this was another 1920 trip scouting for trapping cabin sites, August was thirty-four and his hair had begun to recede. Who took the photo? The Kodak may have had a timer, but it doesn't look as if August had a long flex, as Francis Barrow did during the same period, allowing him to take photos that included himself. With money and leisure to travel all summer, then boat back to the comfort of a Sidney winter house, Barrow was touring: drawing and photographing pictographs, chatting up the locals and documenting logging shows. *His* trip up Bute was a day

August, standing in the longboat, shows off a good catch so a companion can take the shot.
Pansy Eddington collection

cruise aboard the steamer *Cassiar* only as far as the Orford River.[15] August, in his dugout and on foot, was imaging a deeper upcoast world he'd learned to move through out of stark necessity, but which, approached with extensive wilderness skills, could produce an abundance he liked to display. He was ready for a permanent family move up into Bute.

Once August located his trapping cabin sites, he and Zaida began the floathouse move from the Nodales Channel/Shoal Bay area into the inlet. Another set of images indicates how their first house was set up so it could be dismantled, moved onto floats and towed to a bay where a handlogging licence had been obtained.

Two cougar hounds on the floathouse before move to Bute, early 1920s. *August Schnarr photo. Image MCR 20447-93 courtesy of the Museum at Campbell River*

One of the photos features two recumbent cougar hounds. The dog on the left lounges on a wide plank set on the lower skid logs. The photo shows how the smaller building, upper left, is skidded on top of the cross logs below the shack to the right, thereby creating their often-photographed internal porch.

In another shot the smaller building has been slid left and turned so it could be winched on or off the logs beached in front. Since August is walking behind the big logs needed for a float, Zaida is likely the photographer. Washing is hung behind the outhouse on the right, and rising smoke indicates nothing is going anywhere right then, May 28, 1924.

Another photo in Pearl's *Cougar Companions* has the floathouse complex at Fawn Bluff, and a later photo places the four buildings onshore at Schnarr's Landing below the garden. "Big garden," Pearl said. "Grew raspberries and loganberries. Canned everything."

Proud of their family, Zaida and August posed with Pearl and new baby Marion against neatly stacked firewood. Then the three girls, a little older, hug Jack McPhee's puppies and a cat on the Landing beach below the distinctive small building.

A photo taken after Einer Johnson logged August's land east of the buildings shows the top

Below: A note on the negative says, "Moving buildings, Nodales Channel." *Zaida Schnarr photo. Image MCR 20447-24 courtesy of the Museum at Campbell River*

Top: Schnarr's Landing garden.
August Schnarr photo. Image MCR 14388 courtesy of the Museum at Campbell River

Middle left: August, Marion and Pearl.
Zaida Schnarr photo. Image MCR 20447-32 courtesy of the Museum at Campbell River

Middle right: Zaida, Marion and Pearl.
August Schnarr photo. Image MCR 20447-30 courtesy of the Museum at Campbell River

Below: Marion, Pansy and Pearl at the Landing with Jack McPhee's puppies and a cat, 1927/28.
August Schnarr photo. Image MCR 14408 courtesy of the Museum at Campbell River

Logging done by Einer Johnson and his steam donkey at the Landing. Animal shed with waterline in the foreground.
August Schnarr photo. Image MCR 6700 courtesy of the Museum at Campbell River

Schnarr trapping cabin, Homathko Valley.
August Schnarr photo. Image MCR 6703 courtesy of the Museum at Campbell River

Beryl Johnson and Zaida Schnarr, c. 1928–1931. *August Schnarr photo. Image MCR 14421 courtesy of the Museum at Campbell River*

corner of the garden, perhaps potato hills, and the waterline to the rabbit, mink and marten shed. It must date from the 1928–1932 period when the lease was certified, the garden established and August could log his land.

While Einer logged, his wife, Beryl, sat with Zaida behind a very dead bear draped over a log. I shift the photo to begin a suit of dead-creature images I line up under August's photograph of one of the Homathko Valley trapping cabins he used each winter. The camera's lack of focal depth makes the women seem mobile and cheerfully chatting behind the inert, sharp-focused bear.

My friend Esther, looking over my shoulder, labelled this photograph "The Quick and the Dead." She pushed a different print below it. "This is it," she said. "This is the cover of your book about Schnarr."

A cougar pelt, the head propped on a shake wedged into a chair back, is hung over a pole suspended so the legs almost walk along the deck of the porch. "Dead and alive," my conceptually minded pal titled it. Schooled in theories of photography that posit a photo as a vanished moment endlessly recurring, she saw this photo, staged to animate the expired, as illustrating that duality. More schooled in Schnarr family history, I questioned what kind of cougar August had in mind, the hunted or the hugged?

"Consider the image from a position within the backwoods economy," I proposed. "In those

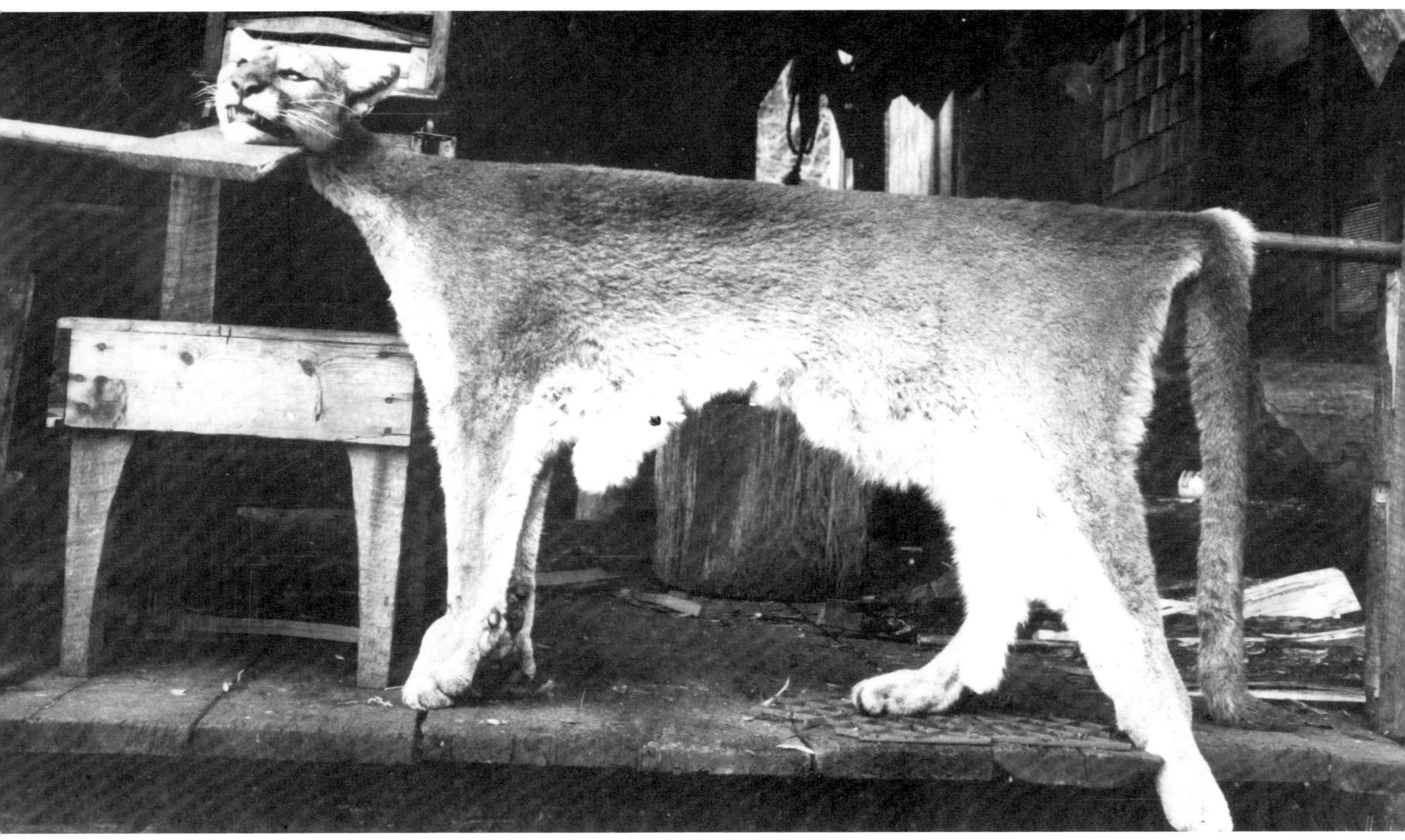

Cougar pelt.
August Schnarr photo. Image MCR 20447-41 courtesy of the Museum at Campbell River

days you had to turn in the cougar nose or ear to receive the bounty, but could sell the pelt. Although August said cougar pelts were not much valued then, according to his 1927 accounts he received forty dollars for one from Mr. Tipton at Surge Narrows Store. A trophy hunter he guided might pay more for a complete head to mount with the pelt. Perhaps that was what August had prepared, what he wanted to show."

"What's a bounty?" Esther asked.

"Vancouver Island once supported the largest and most aggressive cougar population in North America. Until 1958," I say, "cougars were labelled vermin, and the government bounty once rose to forty dollars for each nose turned in—a lot of cash during the Depression. The phenomenal number of animals eradicated through the bounty program reduced predation on domestic animals and deer, animals we wanted for food. Aligning this image with the one of Pearl and Girlie demonstrates our complicated attitude toward animals we hug and feed, those we kill and eat, and some we kill, don't eat, stuff, mount, admire and sometimes wear. We *can* become prey.

"During one solitary hunt, August climbed up cliffs high above the entrance to the Homathko River to hunt goats. A black bear charged him and August almost fell off the cliff. He reached for the Luger he kept in the top of his backpack and shot the bear. But he was puzzled by the charge as bears usually avoided him. Then he saw there was more than one bear and they were trying to run goats off the cliff. Stripped down to his white long johns due to the heat of the day, he'd been mistaken for a goat."

August's staged game photos suggest he is advertising available Bute furs to buyers like Pappas Furriers on Granville Street in Vancouver, whose letters to him regarding prices are in the Schnarr fonds. "If your skins are Mink—we can use them from $6.00–$7.00 per skin, but it relies a lot on the colours," T. Pappas wrote in February 1940. "I would suggest you ship your skins here and I want to assure you that you will have nothing to worry about, we will allow you every dime that is in them." Pappas was also interested in "extra large" and "large" marten skins ($18.00–$22.00), "smalls" ($12.00–$13.00) and beaver, for which they'd pay "up to $30.00 for fine, large, good skins."

"I never went up the Homathko trapping with August," Pearl had said, "but I did go up the Southgate on a way into the Interior in the '30s. There was a cabin. Dad's trapline was seven hours in and out. It was Marion who went up the river valleys with him the most, went up in the series of longboats, Dad's canoes. Marion was a good shot, always carried a gun."

August also guided a government survey party up the Homathko in 1928–1930, and in 1929 he and Charlie Rasmussen would spend three months trapping for marten up that river.

INTERLUDE II

THE WIND HAS ALWAYS BLOWN

Charlie Rasmussen's Bute wax.
Judith Williams photo

When my *High Slack: Waddington's Gold Road and the Bute Inlet Massacre of 1864* was published in 1995, I received a call from Charlie Rasmussen's daughter Sylvia Ives, inquiring about my reference to Bute wax based on a paper by M.Y. Williams in the *Transactions of the Royal Society of Canada.*[16] Williams wrote that the balls of Bute wax, which Pearl said August had loaded into his canoe, rolled in "scow-loads" along the shores of Bute Inlet and collected around log booms during frigid weather in the 1950s. When the inlet temperature ameliorated, the substance melted and could not be found. Williams claimed Bute wax was a plant-based derivative. Sylvia wanted to show me her father's treasured sample of this inlet substance, as well as a diary he kept of his 1929 winter trapping trip up the Homathko Valley with August Schnarr.

With the map from Charlie's tiny, handwritten record opened on the table of the café where we met, Sylvia and I followed him and August up the Homathko toward the BC Interior. The diary entries vividly described the difficulties of boating and trekking up the wild river, and of snow camping to trap marten in the alpine.

Then Sylvia reached into her bag and pulled out a small bottle of a viscous golden substance that flowed imperceptibly down, coating the glass. Bute wax was gorgeous! I wanted to eat it or rub it all over my body. Although I had noted its existence, this was my first sighting of something I came to feel stood for the inlet. No one had seen it for years.

"Dad had three samples of the Bute wax material you wrote about," Sylvia said. "I have one more sample like this, but another more transparent one has disappeared. I'd say 98 per cent of the wax we had came from the water. It collected around the log booms of Len Parker, August Schnarr's cross-inlet neighbour in Bear Bay, where it was easiest to get. Everyone thought it was a local form of petroleum. Dad was involved with trying to get samples analyzed, and he and Len were dissatisfied with a Dr. Jain they'd transported up-inlet sometime between 1965 and '70. My brother has a map of the location of a smouldering stump impregnated with the material. The locals felt it indicated some kind of onshore source that Munday McCrae, Parker, Ed Adkin, the Moulds, Schnarr and that handsome devil Jack McPhee, all living up Bute during that period, searched for. He wouldn't let me bring it."

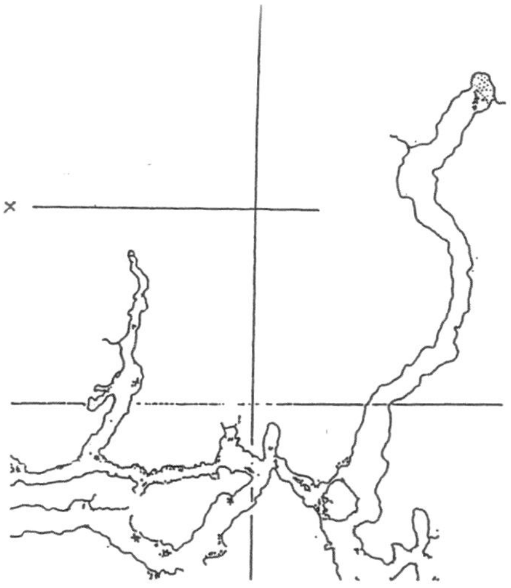

Sylvia's aureate jar fired my senses. It was easy to imagine Len Parker and Laurette, the third Mrs. Parker, who Sylvia vividly described as the "Dolly Parton of Bute Inlet," wallowing in it under the stuffed sea lion said to thrust out into the living room of their Bear Bay cabin. Paired with Charlie's diary map of the Homathko Valley expedition, it gave me the same physical rush I got in Bute Inlet's vast spaces, where I was awed by the sudden "Bute" wind, the bottomless anchorage problem, Bear Bay's luminous jade waves and the astounding Homathko waterway to peak mountain extremes. The wax and diary were time bombs, opening tracks in dozens of directions. Sylvia quickly saw I was hooked on the inlet mystique and left Charlie's wax sample with me to get its contents analyzed.

FROM JOHNSTONE'S ROUGH CHART
231, Part 4, on Ac1

x ---------------- = latitude at head
50° 43' 12"

James Johnstone's survey chart, 1792.
Map by James Johnstone

Over the following years, as I learned more and more about August Schnarr, the girls and the cougars, I realized Bute wax, the mystery of its substance, origin, storage and performance, created the very kind of puzzle August thrived on. According to Charlie's diary, August used his trapping trips to tease out coastal systems and follow their threads. Was that stone platform he found part of Waddington's road? Where *was* that on-land, grease-soaked, burning stump the old-timers thought *had* to be connected to some petroleum source?

Everybody speculated about why this useful substance was found in Bute Inlet and nowhere else on the coast, but Bute is exceptional in many ways. Second longest of the West Coast fiords, Bute is surrounded by mountains that rise precipitously from the water and plunge steeply 300 to 650 metres (1,000 to 2,100 feet) below the surface. The 80-kilometre (50-mile) channel regularly becomes a 4-kilometre-wide (2.5 miles) wind tunnel. Blowing down the Homathko Valley off Mt. Waddington, the highest peak completely within British Columbia, the wind is so famously ferocious its blow is known as a "Bute" in English and Xwe7xw to the Homalco, who say, "We have always lived here and the wind has always blown."[17] A Homalco story of the

wind's source blames Raven for everything. Tired of the strong wind that makes it difficult for them to travel, Raven, Heron, Seagull, Crow and Grebe journey to the northern country, where Wind-maker lives with his wife and son. Heron kills Wind-maker and his wife, but Raven takes the young boy home as a slave. According to Homalco elder Noel George Harry, "Today there are many winds because Raven took Wind-maker's boy home with him."[18]

Xwe7xw is also the Homalco People's name for Mt. Waddington. Located 60 kilometres (37 miles) up the Homathko River Valley, at 4,019 metres (13,186 feet high) it is the tallest mountain entirely in British Columbia. The Homalco believe Xwe7xw is the keeper of the infamous north Bute wind. Don't make fun of him or throw things in his direction or the "Bute" will blow. Xwe7xw was an important Homalco hunting ground for mountain goat, bear and deer. The magnificent 120-metre (400-foot) rock spire flanking the peak may have inspired their belief that the mountain was once a man who frequently wandered around. His wife, daughter and dogs are the individual peaks on the southwest side of Southgate Peak on the east side of the inlet. A dog-shaped stone, now under the road, reportedly graced the Southgate's bank.

The abrupt Bute temperature drops that allowed Bute wax to surface and harden are attested to in the story of a tug that arrived in Waddington Harbour to pick up a boom during the 1950s. It was so suddenly struck by a glacial wind that an ice carapace formed all over one side. In order not to capsize the tug, the captain had to release the boom and periodically turn the boat end to end, running south in reverse half the time so the ice buildup evened out.

The 120-metre spire alongside the main summit of Mt. Waddington, photographed by legendary British mountaineer Doug Scott when he and Rob Wood climbed Waddington in 1978.

Nothing small ever happens in Bute. The wind blows the hardest, the temperature drops the quickest and furthest. The whole place is Guinness World Record material.

James Johnstone's 1792 survey for Captain Vancouver correctly indicates Bute Inlet takes a jog west after Schnarr's Landing. At Purcell Point it rounds out to its widest point at Bear Bay, where the wax seemed to collect. Where the inlet narrows to the Waddington Harbour shallows, copious runoff from three glacier-fed rivers deposits silt and creates a layer of fresh water 9 metres (30 feet) deep, extending 50 kilometres (30 miles) south. This may have caused the wax's accumulation at Bear Bay.

Upper Bute Inlet and Homathko Valley.

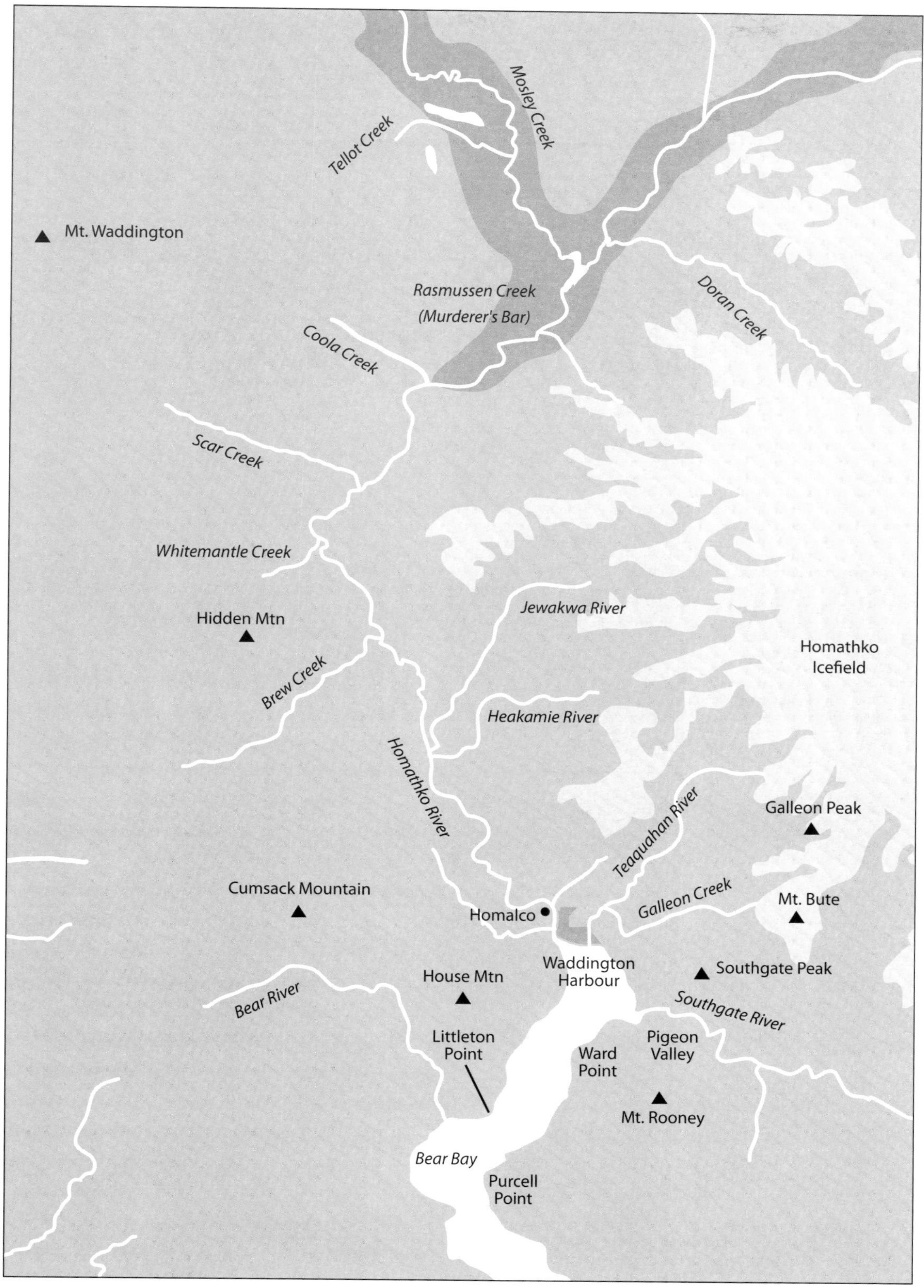

3

UPSTREAM AGAINST THE CURRENT

Upper Homathko Valley, looking downstream from a point four miles below Tatlayoko Lake, August 1928. *"Water Power Investigations: Report on Taseko–Chilko–Homatho project," page 1023, photo 59*[19]

The Homathko, one of the major rivers of the Coast Mountains of British Columbia, penetrates the range from the Chilcotin Plateau to enter the sea at the head of Bute Inlet, opposite the mouth of the Southgate River. Major Cecil Harlow Edmond explored this central coast area and the Chilcotin to find saleable timber and other resources. Around 1920 he informed the BC government that, because of a significant elevation difference, there was hydroelectric potential if Chilko Lake were diverted westward from Franklyn Arm via Tatlayoko Lake into the Homathko River.[20]

Edmond Creek, flowing northwest into the south end of Chilko Lake, is named after Major Edmond, whose family has owned Lot 108 at the head of Bute Inlet since this time.

Since Edmond's report, the 5,335-square-kilometre (2,059-square-mile) drainage area of the two rivers has tantalized hydro engineers. When a government hydro survey was sent up the Homathko in the summer of 1928, chief hydraulic engineer F.W. Knewstubb noted that "Mr. August Schnarr [who] had trapped and hunted the lower part of the [Homathko] West Fork . . . gave the party the benefit of his experience." August ferried the group up the Homathko and outlined the route a survey party could take to the Interior.

Knewstubb edited the survey report, "1928–1930 Water Power Investigation of the Taseko–Chilcotin–Homathko," which contains location photos, panoramic vistas and elegant hand-drawn maps. A handful of photos from August's negatives, alongside some spectacular photos from the surveyors, create a subset of the Schnarr family taxonomy. One survey photo shows a narrow chasm up the Homathko canyon, a necessary crossing on Waddington's route to the gold fields, and one a hydro survey would have to consider. August had found that crossing the river on a tree felled for the purpose made the up-valley route considerably shorter. In the related West Fork (Mosley Creek) image, men move packs along a log over a river while holding on to a rope guide-rail, something August ordinarily disdained.

On the survey party's return from the Chilcotin, the group ran low on supplies. Knewstubb must have come down to the inlet with, or to get, August, as he wrote in his report:

> An arrangement was made whereby Schnarr, with an assistant [Charlie Rasmussen] for his long riverboat, and Knewstubb, Chief Field Engineer, forming . . . a "rescue party," met the survey

Left: Canyon, West Fork of the Homathko River. *"Water Power Investigations: Report on Taseko–Chilko–Homatho project," page 1226, photo 72*[21]

Right: West Fork, Homathko River. *"Water Power Investigations: Report on Taseko–Chilko–Homatho project," page 1226, photo 65*[22]

August's expert handling of backcountry hazards contributed to the wilderness reputation that led pioneering coastal mountaineers Don and Phyllis Munday to seek his advice. For their May 1926 first assault on Xwe7xw, then known as Mystery Mountain (now Mt. Waddington), August laid out the climbers' route to his trapping cabin and the glacier up which they must travel. Don Munday reported their upriver difficulties with 40-acre logjams, river quicksand and the waterway crossings August habitually made that defeated most folk.[23]

"Oh! Those glacier creeks are wild," Phyllis wrote late in life. "Carrying a sixty-pound pack on your back on a log over a wild glacier creek and the end of the log was just on the other shore and the water was so swift it was shaking the log! Oh, and to stay on the log with your pack on your back and get across . . . well, there wouldn't have been a hope in the world of course, if anybody had ever got into it."[24]

Chief hydraulic engineer F.W. Knewstubb setting out on the 1928 survey.
Frank Swannell photo[25]

party working down from the Lake—near the Forks. Provisions, tobacco, boots and clothes (stated in order of necessity) were about all done for. Schnarr helped out considerably by baking bread in his famous outdoor bakery which, with fish caught in the river, was about all the party had to live on for the last few days. The party travelled downstream, walking or relaying ahead with the longboat, to Gilkey's and Adkin's logging camps near the mouth of the river, where they were all well fed and well treated generally.

According to Charlie Rasmussen: "Schnarr and I met Knewstubb, Chief Engineer of a survey party, in 1927–28, at the point where the main 1860s massacre occurred [and] escorted them out. We brought in about 800 pounds of supplies by canoe to the survey gang."[26] Charlie noted that "Murderer's Bar," the location of the killings, would be shown as Rasmussen Creek on maps.

August's input allowed the surveyors to record evidence of Waddington's 1860s gold road. The road crew had built a log bridge across the Homathko Canyon, and the surveyors photographed what they thought were its remains, as well as relics from the cabin belonging to the ferryman killed at "Murderer's Bar" in 1864, near where August built his trapping cabin.

The intensity of the Homathko River current, caused by the canyon constriction, has always made boat passage all but impossible. When trying to push the road through in the 1860s, Waddington's crew found building anything from the lower end unfeasible and constructed a pack road that switchbacked up from just south of the canyon, over the 2,000-foot rise and down.

A photo taken in 1875 by Charles Horetzky, after the road was abandoned, shows where Waddington's crew drilled holes along the canyon side, cemented in steel pins and cantilevered a track out for the mules. Mules? You remember that shoe Carl Larson found, which Glen Macklin

Knewstubb included a photo of "Schnarr's B.C. Bakery" in the survey report. Pearl proudly told me August was unique in making sourdough bread in camp by building an oven that sat over the fire. BC Archives identifies the location of this photo as Orford Bay, dates and locations being notoriously unstable in the memory theatre.
August Schnarr negatives

Remains of Waddington's road bridge near bottom of canyon, Homathko River, 1928.
Image A-01578 courtesy of the Royal BC Museum and Archives

The Great Canyon of the Homathko, proposed Damsite #G.2.

"Water Power Investigations: Report on Taseko–Chilko–Homatho project," page 1033, photo 94[28]

Remains of Waddington's road after a flood, looking downstream from the north, 1875.
Charles Horetzky photo, Vancouver Public Library 8545

brought me? Carl says elements of the pack road on dry land up over the canyon can still be traced, even after 130 years, because the trees grow so slowly. He based his search for remaining evidence of the road and the massacre in the canyon on a statement from the Homalco man Qwittie, cook for the foreman of the road crew, who testified at the trial of the arrested Tŝilhqot'in concerning the killing of the crew.[27] Carl didn't get a reading with his metal detector until he came to a very old cedar near the trail. He dug up a broken iron pot and found an axe head that an expert later authenticated as having been made in 1850 by Collins and Co. Climbing up a rock slide at the top of the canyon above Waddington's ferry, Carl pulled rock away so it wouldn't fall on a man behind him and found two new mule shoes wired together. He speculated that after killing the ferryman, the Tŝilhqot'in warriors smashed the pot and took the shoes, which they later threw away.

Knewstubb's survey party climbed up over that canyon and took a remarkable photo down into the Homathko gorge, where they proposed situating Damsite #G.2.

The canyon remains a challenge when moving upriver to the northwest and is difficult to traverse downstream. In the 1970s a group intending to kayak down to the inlet was dropped above the canyon, but members found they had to rock-climb through it sideways, trailing their crafts on leads. The canyon stymied the progress of Waddington's road, as bridges and tracks were blown out over the winters. The 1930s hydro project was shelved due to what Knewstubb admitted would be unjustifiable construction expense for the financial return.

Even today the area's extreme weather and the seasonal variation of Homathko River flow may impede proposed run-of-river hydro projects. Although the Homathko's volume peaks in July due to snowpack melt, disgorging the third-largest flow of water of any river in the province, a flowmeter above Homathko Camp indicates it can be reduced to 10 per cent of that in

Some of the twelve marten pulled off traps in one day, Homathko River. From Charlie Rasmussen's diary. *August Schnarr photo. Image MCR 14415 courtesy of the Museum at Campbell River*

winter. An unusually hot day or a massive rainfall, winter or summer, can send the river many feet higher in hours. When we foolishly anchored our 60-foot seiner *Adriatic Sea* off the river mouth near Scar Creek Logging's booms in late summer, a heavy overnight rainfall raised the river so much that, combined with a high tide, it lifted our anchor. By morning *Addy*, with more luck than we deserved, had drifted safely into the open arms of boom logs. A couple of years later a sudden melt caused a glacier lake to collapse; a 20-foot wall of water reportedly swept down the Homathko. Don Munday wrote that "the valley is an ongoing cycle of destruction and reclamation."[29]

To get into this volatile wilderness to trap, August had learned to leave his canoe below the canyon, follow bear trails up above the river, and climb up into the alpine and onto glaciers in winter—sometimes alone, at least once with Rankin, occasionally with Charlie Rasmussen, later with Marion. One Cortes Island visitor, Doug Dewar, said he and August were on a steep bear trail, one behind the other, in the 1950s when a bear came roaring toward them. When August shot it, they had to step sharply aside as it rolled wildly downhill, threatening to bowl them over.

Charlie Rasmussen, age nineteen. *Charlie Rasmussen collection*

Pearl had told me that the winter after the survey, Charlie Rasmussen and August, desperate for cash, teamed up to trap marten.[30] Frigid winter conditions developed the thick marten pelts furriers marketed as Canadian sable. I found a photo of a string of pine marten in Pearl's *Cougar Companions* album and in Charlie Rasmussen's 1929 trapping diary file that Sylvia loaned me.[31] The two men trekked up the Homathko River and into uninhabited territory behind Mystery Mountain from October 1 to mid-December.

In a letter to Dorothy McAuley, Charlie wrote: "We ran trap line from foot of Tiedemann Glacier in many branch lines around mountains and valleys, 60 miles total and got 85 fur marten and weasels in 4 weeks. Additional 2 months was used in relaying supplies in and returning December 20, 1929. The Waddington Trail which had been linked through from head of Bute Inlet to Tatla Lake was still visible in parts, but not of any assistance to us as the 2 canyon cliff roads were destroyed over many years by weather conditions."

Charlie's diary map (see page 53) traces the trappers' route from Bute Inlet (top), along the Homathko Valley to two lean-tos on the north side of the Homathko and a cabin above Coula

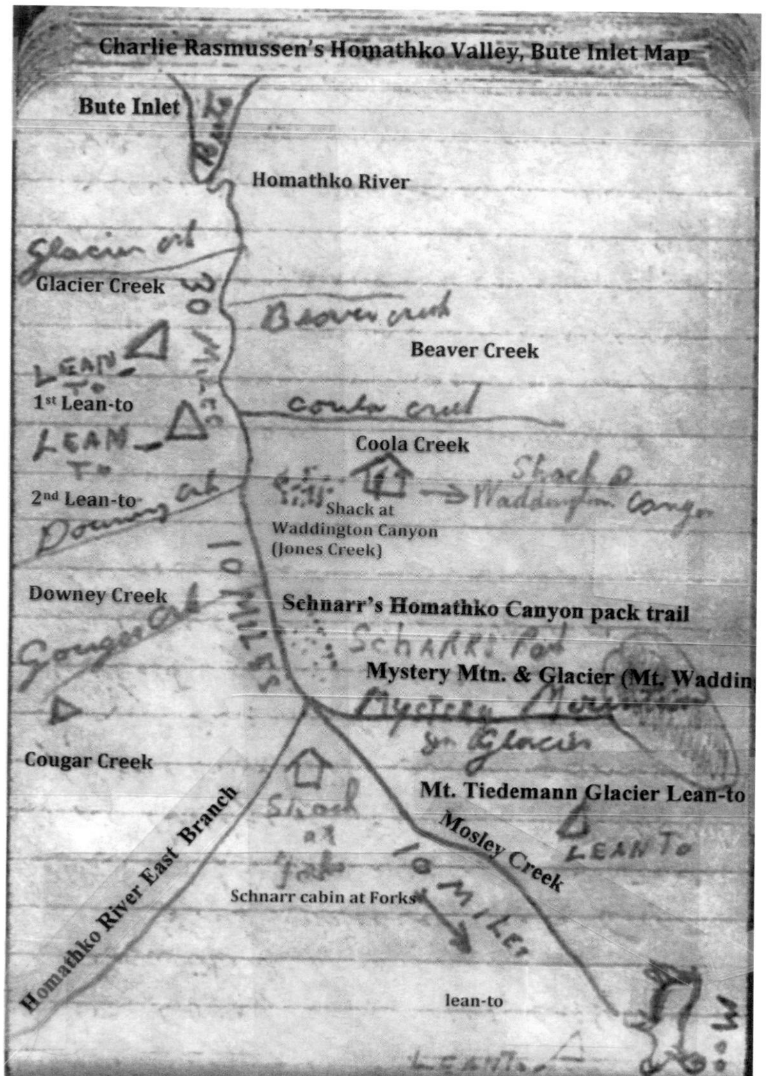

Above: Pine marten.

© jimcumming88 / Adobe Stock

Left: Charlie Rasmussen's diary, 1929.

Charlie Rasmussen collection

Creek. They left the canoe, blocked up out of the flow, at Jones Creek. The map indicates a trapping cabin above the Homathko Forks and a 10-mile trip up the West Fork (Mosley Creek) of the Homathko to a lean-to at Mt. Tiedemann Glacier, then another 10 miles toward Tŝilhqot'in territory to another lean-to and a moose sighting. Trekking up the East Branch to Tatlayoko Lake, an obvious route on a map, is described as a tougher journey by those who've tried it.

The energetic Charlie, twenty-three, raised at the Rasmussen Bay family homestead north of Lund, writes of the cold and hardships during the trip with remarkable good humour. A Schnarr photo in Charlie's Bute file shows a pile of gear and a clinker-built rowboat, perhaps his up-inlet transport, on the south-facing beach at Schnarr's Landing. His diary begins:

> October 1, Tuesday. Left Schnarr's 1:00, arrived mouth of river 3:30. Camped at Gilkie's Camp 5:30. Started next morn 8:00. Arrived Beaver Creek 5:30. Red sky in the morning so will use lean-to tent tonight.
>
> Oct 3rd, Thursday. Started to rain last night and has poured down since. Divided load in two. Took first load as far as Schnarrs lean-to, which is in an ideal spot under huge cedars.

> Brought up second load after dinner. Schnarr's watch 3 hrs., faster than mine. Do not know which is right.

By October 4 they'd canoed 500 pounds of supplies 10 miles up to the next lean-to below Downy Creek. The river was so wild they had a few close shaves, and Charlie writes of many aches and sprains, but he also saw four bears and two wolves on the river bar, and a few seagulls 25 miles upriver from the head of the inlet.

On the 7th, Charlie took "a wild and wooly" canoe ride back downriver to the first lean-to. Poling the canoe alone against the current, it took him seven hours to bring supplies back up. His diary lists the many provisions they brought and broke up into separate numbered packs for different locations and time periods, but in spite of the hundreds of pounds of supplies they carried, they still had to hunt and fish to supply enough protein for such packing and poling. On the 8th, Charlie caught seven Dolly Varden trout in an hour. He cut wood and baked bread to go with the trout and boiled potatoes. After tea, pilot bread and jam, he went to swamp out an easier trail over Homathko Canyon (which was then known as Waddington Canyon). After that they'd be on foot.

From Charlie's diary:

> October 9, Wed. Took pack over to great divide. Cached it by old surveyor's camp. Found Bear had opened can and spoiled coffee. All set for tomorrow's hike. Each pack 60–70 lbs.

On the 10th the travellers cut trail from their cache along what August called the "Caribou Road to the top of Great Divide," Waddington's intended route. Charlie fell over a sleeping bear on the way back to camp, but even without a gun they scared off its grumpy attack. August washed clothes.

The Homathko Valley from Great Divide.
August Schnarr photo. Image MCR 20447-74 courtesy of the Museum at Campbell River

> October 11th, Left cabin at 7 am. Arrived cache 2 pm. Stopped for lunch at Giant Rock, Saw three goats across canyon. Highest point of trail over divide 1500–2000 feet above sea level. Schnarr still trying to pick up loose ends of Caribou Trail. Woke up one night and found mice busy chewing my hair.

Giant Rock was a huge granite slab located right on the trail that must be followed over the canyon to get farther upriver. They deposited packs there and headed back downriver to relay more supplies. On the 12th, Charlie noted:

> Back at [lower] cabin at 3:30. Had shot of coffee and fixed canoe and had supper. Chased three raccoons up cedar tree 50 feet from cabin. Two rotten trout there that they were eating. Puff puff! Just sneaked up on one raccoon . . . made a dash at it and chased it for a hundred feet or so into [a patch of] Devils Club.

Man holding a rifle against a granite slab near Waddington trail. *August Schnarr photo. Image MCR 20447-47 courtesy of the Museum at Campbell River*

Back at Giant Rock with supplies, the trappers cut wood and dried their clothes. Heavy rain had raised the river's level three feet in two days and turned it into a muddy torrent. To continue travelling close to the river they had to cut a new, higher trail above the Homathko that took them by what they called "Castle Rock." The noise of the river tearing loose huge logjams, and the ceaseless reports of boulders striking against each other in the torrent, reminded August of gunfire in the fields of France. Dinner was rice and raisins, pilot bread, jam and tea; supper and breakfast, beans and more beans!

> Oct. 17, Thursday. No rain today, saw sun for a min. Good signs this eve for good weather. Schnarr stayed in camp and baked bread, while I took three packs up to Castle Rock. Great excitement 1 p.m. Hear airplane and rushed madly for a clear lookout but could not see it. Schnarr saw it upriver eight miles circling East and West Forks. Great curiosity about what it's up there for. River dropped one foot today. Schnarr found horseshoe, souvenir of 1863 Caribou pack train.

On the 18th the men moved camp from Giant Rock to Murderer's Bar, half a mile above Castle Rock, and made a shaky bridge around Castle Rock. It was rainy, and the two were gloomy until they got a tent up and the big fire going. August vowed to get moose, mowich (deer) or goat the next day.

On the 19th, while August went hunting, Charlie took three packs over the pole bridge and cut a trail to Crevice Bluff. He planned to do what he called "a Blondin," carrying packs across the 300-foot Homathko chasm at Crevice Bluff.[32] A Homalco story identifies one such upriver chasm crossing as a test of courage involving a long run, a giant leap and an essential fall as far forward as possible. Failing the latter necessity, one leaper slid down to the bottom of the canyon with not much left of his hands.[33] August's solution was to fall a giant fir across the chasm. On the 20th, Charlie carried eight packs to Crevice Bluff and sensibly built a ladder beside the log to improve the crossing. On the 21st, he moved ten packs over the bluff, noting: "Blondin stunt a nerve-wracking experience. No place for anybody with a weak heart."

The trappers then organized two packs for the heaviest day of packing yet, to "The Forks," where the Homathko branches right toward Tatlayoko Lake and left to become Mosley Creek. Crazy for meat, they hunted ptarmigan and goat, and on the 24th built a bridge across the Tiedemann Glacier runoff while up to their waists in ice-cold water. Charlie shot two small rainbow trout at Lorin Creek and saw coyote tracks on the river bar. On the 28th everything in camp froze. They brought more packs up from Crevice Bluff, and on the 30th Charlie smoked marten traps to remove human scent, while August hunted for more palatable meat.

> Oct. 31st, Thursday. Threatened snow but cleared off in afternoon. Took last pack and lunch kit up today. Two packs over Grizzly Creek to cabin. Nothing left but shoelaces dragging.
>
> Nov. 2, Saturday. Fine clear weather. Worked around cabin all day making bunk table, smoking bacon, baking bread. Mice celebrated our arrival by galloping all over my head during the night and eating rolled oats. Set patent mousetraps tonight.
>
> Sunday. Went up to Lorna Lake. Schnarr shot goat. Lots of trout jumping in lake. Used old raft on lake that is approximately 1/2 mile long.

The trappers undertook a formidable four-day hike up the West Fork of the Homathko. They spotted moose tracks and a big beaver dam and house. Camping out on November 7, they "set fire to a huge cedar that was hollow to the top and had been used by bears for winter quarters. Fire so huge and hot we had to take to woods til it fell completely burnt up. Spent another nightmare night by open fire."

Crossing a glacier on November 8, Charlie was awed by spectacular ice caverns, sunken crevice lakes and rocks piled hundreds of feet in the air. On the 9th he climbed back up to Lorna Lake, below the Homathko's East Branch, to check traps, but the raft had drifted away and he

August Schnarr's main cabin at the Forks between the East and West Branches of the Homathko River. Remains of the supine roof, found by Carl Larson in 1990s, indicate August roofed the cabin with split cedar inside up with spaces capped by inside-down cedar.
August Schnarr photo. Image MCR 14430 courtesy of the Museum at Campbell River

had to climb up over a mountain and back down to the lake to retrieve it. He packed 100 pounds of goat meat to camp while August built cages for live marten he planned to take home to breed.

On November 10 they improved the cabin, putting in windows and adding more chinking. August set to work baking bread.

On November 11 the trappers headed down to the Cougar Creek lean-to in snow and hiked the 7.5 miles back to camp with part of a goat to make a mulligan stew they followed with tea, cocoa, bread, jam and prunes. They were always hungry!

By Saturday, November 16, they were back at the Forks, hoping for clear, cold weather. Checking traps up the last branch of Mosley Creek, they crossed the river twice on a pole bridge, but waded four other streams, with icy water up to their waists.

> Nov. 19, Tuesday. Still clear and freezing. Mystery Mountain looking like ghost in the moonlight. Took sashay up left side [Tiedemann] glacier and got a big, four point buck. 300 lbs. or more. Hot Dog! Some pack.

Charlie and August took turns going up the East and West Branches of the Homathko and onto the glaciers checking traps. Charlie was stiff and sore after another bitterly cold night sleeping out by the fire.

> Nov. 25th, Monday. Heavy Fog. Went up glacier part way. Schnarr working around line to meet me at lean-to.

The next day Charlie went back up the glacier in fog to meet August at the sunken lake. The cracked ice was pushed 10 feet up onto the shore so they were forced to detour around it.

On the back of this photo, Charlie wrote, "Schnarr getting ready for a feast. Homathko River, Bute Inlet, Nov 18, 1929. The main method of fishing was shooting the trout with rifles esp. in winter." August's canoe stretches along the riverbank behind him.
Charlie Rasmussen photo, August Schnarr negatives. Image MCR 11642 courtesy of the Museum at Campbell River

Above left: Mystery Mountain (later named Mt. Waddington). *Doug Scott photo*

Above right: Waddington Glacier, 1978. *Doug Scott photo*

Wednesday. Foggier than ever. Schnarr and I lost for a couple of hours yesterday afternoon but made lean-to all right.

The next day August went to the canyon lean-to and Charlie hiked to the Forks shack via the West Branch. He mixed up a batch of sour-hots (pancakes) and started bread, but the oven collapsed and one loaf fell in the fire.

Dec. 1st, Sunday. Still mild and clear. Schnarr and I sashayed up West Branch. Left him at 12:30 and went to Tiedemann Glacier lean-to. Picked up one trout on way, two more over river.

Wednesday. Heavy fog. Left Giant Rock 8:05. Arrived cabin [below Homathko Canyon] three hours forty minutes. (Eight miles as the crow flies.) Picked up live female marten today. Didn't have cage so used lunch can. We had a hectic time! Arrived cabin 12:30, tussled with marten and cut her teeth. Roasted front quarter of nanny goat and had great feed. Dried goat carcass and made cages.

On December 8, Charlie and August went downriver below the Homathko Canyon, where they found the flooding river had moved the blockings under the canoe at Jones Creek, though the craft was still there. The wind was howling and everything froze up.

Dec. 9, Monday. Left Waddington cabin [at Jones Creek] 8:30 am. Arrived Forks 1:50. Two hours sleep last night. Caught on fire. Burned to skin on my back and very near took to creek. Just managed to pull off shirt before getting burnt. Also burnt up bag, toque and one mitten in scramble. Oh, what a night!

Tuesday. Slept like log last night. Warm with five blankets, two goatskins and three shirts on. Water freezing three feet from fire. River and creek frozen solid.

The dauntless Charlie trekked farther up the valley to meet August on the 11th.

Arrived river crossing where Schnarr had fire going 11:30 am. Still colder up there and Schnarr looking like old man Bute tonight: overalls sagged at his knees and two inches of ash on his face! Had dinner with him and left for Glacier lean-to while he went back to Chilcotin.

Arrived at Glacier lean-to at 2:10. Cut three logs then axe-handle broke. Heavens! Brr! And, of course, I had forgotten lunch so had beans straight, no soda to take snap away either. Lit fire to big, hollow cedar 20 feet from lean-to. Burned for five hours before it fell and me

Charlie Rasmussen with the same string of fish seen with August on page 57.
August Schnarr photo. Image MCR 20447-35 courtesy of the Museum at Campbell River

watching it like a hawk for fear it would break over camp. Was wishing I had not set fire to it as my wood lasted to 7:30 am, but it was pretty to watch. After it blew a couple of holes through it sounded like giant blower and lit up the woods for 100 yards.

Dec. 12th, Thursday. Ouch! Still colder and what a night! Thank the lord it is one of the last ones out by fire. Left lean-to 8:00 am. Arrived at cabin 1:30. Tired and ravenously hungry. No lunch and lean breakfast. Picked up line, got two Marten, four Weasels.

Over the next few days Charlie pulled the rest of the traps. On Friday the Homathko River and Tiedemann Creek froze over; Saturday it snowed six inches and August arrived "looking like an iceberg."

Dec. 15, Sunday. Taking stock and storing away grub. Leaving in morning for Waddington [Homathko] Canyon.

Careful Charlie listed all his trapping hours in the notebook. The marten had proved plentiful, but by the time he returned to the small community of Lund for Christmas, the stock-market crash had caused the bottom to drop out of the fur market.

Like the Butites' dreams that the Bute wax suddenly appearing under extreme cold and wind conditions was a petroleum product and would make them rich, the fur market failed them. In Charlie's file is a 1929 photo of him with Fred Filander's wife flanking a magnificent cougar. Its bounty nose was worth more than its pelt.

For three decades August continued to climb up into the challenging winter conditions Charlie described to earn what he could. "My father," Marion said, "was an exceptional man. Sometimes he didn't know others weren't." Young Charlie was his match.

In 1937 Charlie Rasmussen was hired by Mr. Richard M. Andrews to supervise construction of a log house on Twin (Ulloa) Islands in Desolation Sound.[34] The Andrews family turned their New York/Tokyo import/export business over to their employees because of the impending war. Having built a log house in Japan, they arrived at the island purchased for them by a Vancouver lawyer and confidently laid out a rambling house form with string.

Charlie hired three expert log-house builders from Quebec and fifteen local woodsmen to construct the house, its furniture and a five-room caretaker's cottage out of island wood. With a horse he got from Fred Thulin, owner of the Lund Hotel on the mainland, they hauled logs to the water and floated them to the big island site. Powell River pioneer John D'Angio told of peeling these logs with a spud, steam-cleaning them, then smoothing them with steel wool and oiling them.[35] Len Parker was hired from Bear Bay to work with D'Angio, improving the view from the house by using a bucksaw and spring rig to lower the hundreds of big stumps left from earlier logging. Charlie took workers up Toba Inlet in his boat *Lauritz* to cut cedar shake bolts from the Big Toba River for the roof. During the eighteen months of construction, Charlie used carrier pigeons to communicate with his mother at Rasmussen Bay.

The Andrewses' daughter, Marion, told me her mother outfitted the enormous log house with furnishings from the Vancouver Hudson's Bay store to complement her father's extensive collection of African animal heads and pelts, and the pole furniture built by Alec North. A great deal of the decor, including a decidedly Canadian moose head, remained where her mother had placed it up to and through the island's ownership by Maximilian, Margrave von Baden. Charlie visited the von Badens, bringing stories of the house construction and the murder of an earlier island owner, a minister mysteriously shot in the jaw through his boat's porthole. The mothers of the margrave and Prince Philip were sisters, and Queen Elizabeth stayed in the house Charlie built.

Charlie Rasmussen and Fred Filander's wife, 1929.
Charlie Rasmussen collection

The drainage entering the Homathko near August's cabin at Murderer's Bar was later named Rasmussen Creek. In 1976 a summer expedition coming down from the Interior, trying to trace Waddington's road, almost came to grief crossing the creek from Tiedemann Glacier, which everyone reports is the hardest part of any trek. Out of supplies, like the 1928 survey crew, they desperately needed to make a Murderer's Bar rendezvous with their downstream food suppliers.

"That creek is deep and fast," one of them reported, "and there are punch-bowl-sized chunks of ice floating down at you. It took twenty

Murderer's Bar, 1875.
Charles Horetzky photo, Vancouver Public Library 8547

minutes to get each person across. Later we were following Rasmussen Creek and doing fairly well. But then it dropped into a sheer rock waterfall about 1,000 feet down this narrow canyon. It was dark and we were working out way down and we just came to a dead end. We put carbineers in and roped ourselves to the rock face for the night."[36]

Although logging roads were pushed up both sides of the Homathko, alder is now reclaiming the land I drove on in 1991, and the territory Charlie and August beavered though in 1929 remains a challenge. In July 2018 the Canadian Exploratory Heritage Society attempted to re-enact the Mundays' first Mt. Waddington assault using handmade period gear. After three weeks of slogging through the wildly tangled Homathko Valley, they discovered they couldn't make it far enough inland to cross the river to reach the glaciers. Like all Bute trekkers, they ran low on food.

Mountaineer Rob Wood, who accomplished the precipitous descent of Rasmussen Creek and was photographed triumphant down on Murderer's Bar, said, "Everything in Bute is extreme!"

INTERLUDE III

HOMATHKO BLUES

It's time for Charlie's lifelong pal Len Parker to come to the front of the stage. A new parallel photo run begins with an image titled "Len's Steam Donkey" from Charlie's trapping diary file. This monster land-boat was able to drag logs and itself through the forest, carrying its own water in the tub that Charlie is inspecting on the right.

Len, an enthusiastic Bute wax collector, was August's nearest and longest-enduring neighbour. He acquired property on the south side of the Bear River in Bute looking across the channel to the grand peaks of Mts. Rodney, Superb and Sir Francis Drake, a spot August had coveted

Len Parker's steam donkey.
Charlie Rasmussen collection

for his homestead. Len established himself as a trapper, prospector, logger and poet during the period when the Schnarrs lived at and around Schnarr's Landing. Len and his wife, Mary, who he called Pearlie, had two sons. After Mary died, his second wife, Anne, a Texas schoolteacher, helped publish his poetry. After they divorced, Len married Laurette in 1959.[37]

Charlie's diary file contains a photo of Len and Betty Vaughn, cook at Ed Adkin's Eva Creek logging camp, riding Len's steel-wheeled logging truck along log rails. Charlie and August had taken Knewstubb's survey crew to be fed at the Eva Creek camp on their return from the 1928 survey.

Top left: Len Parker and Betty Vaughn, Eva Creek, 1928. *Charlie Rasmussen collection*

Top right: Len Parker aboard his boat at Twin Islands, c. 1937. *John Harrison collection*

Below: Butites of the late 1930s lounge on an old gasboat at a log boom when Charlie and Len were working on the Andrews family house at Twin Islands. Charlie Rasmussen standing; Jack McPhee at the left, an unknown man, Len Parker and another unknown person, c. 1937/38. *Charlie Rasmussen collection*

In *Mountain and Forest Philosophy*, published at Stuart Island in 1947, Len evokes the isolated inlet life in the logger-poet rhymes of "Homathko Blues":

Moonlight glistens on the river
Stars look down from Mountains high
Wild geese honk, the while I shiver
Lonely bedtime lullaby.
North wind sweeps down the Homathko
Cold as the summit of Waddington Peak,
Lone wolf howls from a windswept plateau
Life of the wild, forlorn and bleak.
Boom chains snap on log boom swifters,
Snow drifts in through the roof at night,
Glowing red, the oil-drum heater
Cannot subdue the North wind's might.
Northlights dance o'er Mystery Mountain
Eerie the gloom of canyons deep,
The camp grows still as a statue fountain
Lonely and dreaming, at last I sleep.

Len gave the Andrews family a wood-bound, wood-paged copy of his poem "Fir Tree Philosophy" from this book. The text is burned into the pages.

In *Shadows Lay North*, dedicated to Anne, Len introduced one poem with the inscription, "August Schnarr, a friend for many years, has been the author's companion on numerous trips far into unmapped mountain country."

The cover of *Shadows Lay North*, by Len Parker, 1954. *Courtesy of Rita Rasmussen*

August, a mountaineer, rested his pack.
Until his gaze, so intent and afar,
Seemed to be peering beyond things that are.

This sage of mountains, weathered and wise,
What did he see with those age-dimming eyes?

What brought him there above thicket and creek,
Timberline, boulder slide? What does he seek?

Despite Parker's poetic empathy for his neighbour's wilderness fascination, you don't want to imagine that these two lived as sensitive helpmates in the wilderness. Such independent characters always find ways to irritate one another. For some years Len had a tame bear he fed with biscuits to entertain visitors. One day August tied his canoe at Len's dock and strolled to the house. Len, wife and bear came to greet him. The bear, used to being fed, ambled up to August, stood up on its hind feet and put its front paws on his shoulders. August stepped abruptly back, causing the bear's claws to rake his hand. He slugged the bear in the jaw and knocked it out. Nursing his bleeding and bruised hand,

August turned on Len: "The next time he does that I'll shoot it!" He climbed back aboard his canoe and whirled home.

Parker Camp, Bear Bay, 1970.
Vern Logan photo

Although Len moved around for his logging, fishing and trapping work, he was still at Bear Bay when Marion and August were engaged in logging, trapping and animal husbandry in the late 1930s and '40s and when Dennis Walker's grandson, tugboat captain Vern Logan, visited Len in 1970.

After inheriting the Twin Islands house whose construction Charlie and Len had worked on, Max, Margrave von Baden, with his wife, Valerie, youngest granddaughter of the last Hapsburg emperor, and their four children, would boat or fly up Bute Inlet to visit Len and Laurette Parker. Creating an image I treasure, Valerie recalled waiting on Mrs. Parker, a late riser, until she was sufficiently accoutred and made up, apparently a lengthy process.

4

COUGAR TRACKS: THE HUNTED AND THE HUGGED

Pearl and Marion in longboat, Southgate Slough, Bute Inlet, c. 1924/25.
August Schnarr photo. Charlie Rasmussen collection

In early *Cougar Companions* photos, Zaida Schnarr is usually laughing and touching or hugging her girls. She was in the hospital for six months in 1931 after an operation, and following her death from cancer in 1933 at age thirty-one, images of the girls are scarce until the cougars become news. Pansy was coming up to twelve, Pearl ten and Marion about seven when Zaida died.

Pansy described the family's spartan Bute life to Maud Emery, a writer for the Victoria *Colonist*, in 1960, and later in tapes she made for the Campbell River Museum.[38] Like Pearl, she emphasized that she did not know much about their mother as she was boarded out for school at age six, and it was often far too dangerous to travel up the inlet by boat in winter. "I used to go to dances when I was six years old with the lady I lived with in Shoal Bay," she told the Campbell River Museum interviewer. "And she'd put me to bed, when it was time to sleep, behind the piano. That was Mrs. Bryants."

She remembered seeing the Indigenous people living up in Bute in the summer. The family traded them jam for fish. An old couple, Tom and Jenny, who went everywhere in their canoe, "made these baskets for us. This one she made for my Mother . . . made each of us little girls a basket, made of bark.

"In Bute we never knew what it was to go hungry. We canned fruit without sugar—too expensive. Made [our] own smoked fish by [the] root house. We canned tomatoes, carrots, beets, turnips and cabbage. We canned our own meat, made stews. We ate a lot of stew, my dad liked it and it was the easiest for us kids to cook. We were always quite healthy really."

After Zaida died, August, forty-seven, lost everything. Towing his floathouse down inlet, he was hit by a sudden wind at Stuart Island and it sank. The Schnarrs moved to Owen Bay, where there were five or six families and a school.

"Dad tore apart old camp buildings, we straightened nails and August built a house, three rooms and a cellar below. He logged and trapped. Never knew if we'd have gas for the next trip. [We] were struggling and worked hard and steady. It was slim pickings. My dad would never go on relief, no way. He'd fend for himself.

"He taught us to handlog, we bored boomsticks with the old crank auger, we were just as strong as men. We helped him bark logs. We'd run the boat all the time, go and pick a log up, handlogged into the water, we'd run down, start the gasboat up, go on, dog it, tow it in and tie it up on the shore."

Pansy told Emery that after Zaida died and their Aunt Flossie, who had looked after them, left to get married, Flossie's mother-in-law, Mrs. Godkin, became the Owen Bay housekeeper.

August liked to train his cougar dogs around Owen Bay in winter. In the introduction to her *Cougar Companions* albums, Marion describes August setting out from Owen Bay with cougar dogs Rover and Spot on a winter morning in 1934. After boating west out of Okisollo Channel to Barnes Bay, he walked a logging skid road toward Cameleon Harbour on Sonora Island. Fresh snow made tracking easy and he quickly found cougar tracks crossing the road.

"The dogs followed the tracks quietly into the forest, while August continued on his way, listening for the baying of his hounds. After walking through the snow for some distance he came to another set of tracks crossing in the opposite direction. While he was pondering which set of tracks were freshest, he heard the dogs start baying fairly close to the left of the skid road. They didn't run far until it sounded as though they had something at bay. When August made his way to where they were, he saw a large cougar crouched on the limb of a tree. Later, while skinning the beast, he discovered that it had recently been nursing young. So he backtracked to where his hounds had jumped her from under a fallen log and found four hissing kittens."

August took the four handfuls of spotted fur home to his daughters, and Mrs. Godkin cleaned them with damp paper or rag, just as the mother would lick them. Although the local

Top left: Mrs. Godkin feeding one of the cougar kittens at six weeks, c. 1934.
Cougar Companions *album. Schnarr family photo. Image MCR 2006-8 courtesy of the Museum at Campbell River*

Top right: Pansy and Mrs. Godkin with three cougar kittens, c. 1934/35.
Cougar Companions *album. Schnarr family photo. Image MCR 2006-8 courtesy of the Museum at Campbell River*

Right: Pansy, Pearl and Marion with Pat Walsh. Cleo and Leo are six months old.
Cougar Companions *album. Schnarr family photo. Image MCR 2006-8 courtesy of the Museum at Campbell River*

community was captivated by the newborn cougars and supported August's plan to raise them as pets, which had never been done, a few critics thought he was unnecessarily exposing his children to savage animals.

"For the first few days the baby cougars were given milk from a spoon, a method they did not like. Then some kind neighbour brought a nipple and the feedings went much better. On the fourteenth day their eyes started to open. At the age of three weeks one of the two females died. The other three were named Gilmore, Leo and Cleo. Gilmore lived three and a half months."[39]

Cortes pioneer Dunc Robertson was eighteen when he went up Bute to visit the Schnarrs (c. 1934/35). August was away, and Dunc met the housekeeper, who was embarrassed because she was wearing slacks. She said the cougar kittens were ripping her legs. If the cougars were kittens, Dunc must have met Mrs. Godkin.

In a picture of Gilmore, Leo and Cleo at three months, a worried girl holds a big, spotted kitten, while a smiling woman with shiny, waved hair barely contains two spotted furry creatures. This is Pansy with the nurturing Mrs. Godkin. Pansy doesn't even know why she's worried yet, but Mrs. Godkin was becoming fed up with three girls who were not so careful of their hair, and here were kittens to raise as well as girls. It was not long after that "we became bratty, she quit and then I was the mother," Pansy said.

"We made collars for [the cats] out of heavy leather like they use for saddles," Pansy later remembered. "They would break their chains, then hide in the bush and jump out at us when we walked home from school. It would startle us for a minute. Then we'd just take them by the chain and hook up again. When that was enough of that, my dad put heavy anchor chains on them.

"We cooked mash with fish in it for the cougars. They had to eat something, they weren't really well fed but they got nice and fat. We never gave them anything alive, never allowed them to kill anything. They were nice pets, we could pet them and they'd purr just like a cat, and they kept pawing you, don't quit, don't quit. Girlie had a different face to Leo. There's a difference. She's got nice eyes, a kinder look, it's like a tom and a female cat. They didn't like anybody but us three; they didn't like my dad at all. They were just like cats to us, we didn't think of them as anything special, nothing but a bunch of work. We had ten pigs and six dogs and two cougar. The dogs grew up with the cougars. Didn't bother them."[40]

In *Cougar Companions* Marion wrote: "They were kept in the house during the winter and ran about the rooms playing hide and seek. In the spring a wire enclosure was built close to the house and the young cougars spent part of the time there. They were fed in it all the time by then . . . Each would grab their portion and run about snarling savagely, finally settling down to eat. They still slept in the house at night.

"In the summer Leo and Cleo (called Girlie) were put on light chains and had a house of their own for shelter. This was done to safeguard the community livestock. They were close enough together to be able to play and keep each other company . . . they never tangled their chains on anything.

"They made a small, sharp sound for a greeting and purred loudly when they were petted. The cougars were always friendly with the girls, but did not want to be touched by strangers and made their wishes known by hissing. They loved to be played with like a cat and learned easily."

A contemporary view of the Schnarrs comes from an interview with Betty Yerex on another Campbell River Museum tape. When Betty was a very small girl, her father was killed in an accident and her mother, Dorothy, got a job cooking for a logging camp at the head of Bute in "Comack Slough." They'd come up on a steamer to Church House and then up-inlet to a big camp with "lots of food: bear, deer, a hospital and library." Seven miles of rail brought logs down the valley. "August Schnarr was trapping up there," Betty said, "and he came over to camp to visit with his three daughters. His wife was dead then. He used a dugout canoe with a motor to visit."

The cougar cubs were chained to a water tank while Dorothy cooked and sent them away with homemade food. When that camp closed down, Betty said, "a new group came in and Dorothy married the new Camp Super."

It's tempting to speculate that August's visits to the vibrant, independent Dorothy (who I knew as Dorothy Thomas in the 1970s at Refuge Cove) involved courting a new wife. Maybe he was just finding a friend for his girls, but without a new mate, Pansy said, "Our dad raised us like boys. We only had a man's life, we worked like men, he had us handlogging, trapping—we had a pretty rough life."[41]

With Mrs. Godkin gone, the girls shared housekeeping chores. "Pearl was the breakfast cook," Pansy said. "I did lunch and supper and we all did dishes. I was boss more or less. After the move from Bute we spent the winters on Read and every summer we'd go up to Bute again. Every summer holidays we'd spend up there picking berries. We stayed in an open shed, slept on straw. I learned to bake bread over an open fire; we had a gas stove to cook, can fruit with.

"He just had a boatshed left up there and that was where we lived. It was made of poles for

Marion, Girlie and Pearl, c. 1937/38. *August Schnarr photo. Image MCR 15266 courtesy of the Museum at Campbell River*

rafters because he made everything sturdy—we'd climb along those things, no fear in us, chasing wood rats. You know, all we had to do is just roll off that log—we had no way of getting out of there. If we'd broke a leg, an arm, or our neck—nobody'd ever know because we never heard from anybody. We slept outside for six weeks, picking and canning fruit, while he was away fishing up River's Inlet. We had to have it all done when he got back or there's heck to pay. We did get nervous seeing a bear sometime. If you think of kids today living like that when they're 12, 14, 15 years old, it would just shock them to death, but we didn't know any better, we were just used to that way of life."[42]

Behind Pansy and Mrs. G. in the 1935 photo is a logged-off hillside. The Schnarrs killed trees and animals for a living. August killed the kittens' mother for the bounty. He was a logger, and the girls were, as Pearl said, "Loggerettes." In her taped reminiscences, Pansy speaks of the harshness of a trapping life and her ambivalence about killing animals. "When we were a bit older he made us go up his traplines. A two-hour job. He walked for an hour uphill, he'd set ten traps, an hour back. We had to do this by ourselves. I was such a sissy, I was scared the whole time I was gone. Sometimes I'd take my little kitten just to talk to, but I'd be looking behind bushes and scaring myself.

"My Dad liked animals. He liked wildlife, but he had to make his living on it. Killing marten, this is what I hated, when we'd come up to a trap having to kill that little marten that's looking at you. He had his foot in there, he's hurting, and you have to hit him on the head and knock

The Landing.
August Schnarr photo. Image MCR 2006-8 courtesy of the Museum at Campbell River

Previous pages: Leo, Marion, Pansy, Pearl and Girlie, c. 1937/38.
Unknown commercial photographer. Image MCR 15624 courtesy of the Museum at Campbell River

him out and then hang on to his heart 'til it stopped. There's no bruise that way on the flesh. But you know it seems terrible when I think of it now, but it was the way of life then. Shooting deer for meat, we thought that was great sport, and now I think it's the most horrid thing to hear of people out shooting deer.

"Everyone hated the way we were treated, you know, treated like men. I'm glad we weren't men because we would probably have taken a poke at him, but being girls you don't do that. When he took his boat engine apart, we had to be right there so we would know how to fix that Easthope of his. We could run machinery as good as anyone else. We were strong, we used to pull up a hundred feet of that anchor chain, besides a hundred-or-more-pound anchor and a boom chain on it, and we'd pull that up as though we were pulling string."

Pansy said that when they were going to school in Owen Bay, "I would come home during the 10:30 recess, light the fire, stack up the wood, put the kettle on, run back to school, run home at lunchtime and make lunch for my dad and ourselves. The kids would go back. I would do the dishes and run back to school. After school we had chores—dogs to feed, pigs to slop, cougars to look after, pens to clean. There was an acre of garden we had to look after too, then we'd can hundreds of quarts every year."[43]

An undated photo shows the two smaller floathouse buildings, one offset behind the other, in front of the garden. Given the Landing's location in a wide bay on the east shore below a draw running up between Mt. Sir Francis Drake and the "Needles," two-thirds of the way up the inlet, the photo must have been taken from a boat or a float. The water in front of the sheds is calm, which was not often the case, Bute being famously and dangerously windy with regular incoming afternoon swells. The garden stretching uphill has begun to fill out, and the dreamy image suggests a late midsummer afternoon when nothing could go wrong. *Which* summer is the question. Perhaps this image dates from the time after the houses were lost in the tow and the girls spent the summers in Bute alone.

"When we got home to Bute for the summer we'd run all over the boom, and jump in off there and swim around. 'Oh, the water's fine,' we'd say to our dad, 'why don't you come in?' And he'd get in to his knees and couldn't stand it. You get accustomed to it, you're sitting out in the sun all day, getting eaten by horseflies; they're awful up there."

Photographs show how the girls' individual characters became more defined as they matured, but the attitude they display in family photos is slightly different from that in a series taken in 1937–38 for the article by Francis Dickie, a writer living on Quadra Island. A commercial photographer posed the girls on a snowy stage. Pansy and Pearl, overly aware of being represented, confront the camera. Marion holds and perhaps encourages Leo, but the cougars, focused solely on the girls and each other, create a closed pack of five: us here together and you out there. The girls loved those cougars, and the cats were bonded with the girls. It is claimed that cougars are impossible to tame, but Leo and Girlie, imprinted on the girls when they first opened their eyes, knew their names, came when called and could be petted when eating, and the girls could take food away from them.

This image of teenage girls and the cougars—the male cat, Leo, still alive—tells time. The cougars arrived in the winter of 1934; Leo lived for three and a half years, and Girlie for six. The snowy series of photos was used all over the world. An article published in New Zealand produced a pen pal for Pansy and a tempting offer of marriage. "I wouldn't have minded, anything to get away!"

The author of a 1938 article in the *Nashua Telegraph* "Parade of Youth" said the cougars were taught to "jump through the girls' arms, play tug of war, catch food thrown to them." He quoted Pansy saying, "We just let them know who's boss. Anytime we want them to stop doing something we slap them. They quit."

The girls needed to be boss as August was often away. "Dad would be up Chilko Lake trapping for six months in the winter, alone in the snow," Pansy told the Campbell River Museum interviewer. "He made himself cabins all the way through [every 20 miles]. Trap marten inland and mink on the waterfront, otter sometimes. You just took everything you could get . . . Everybody says how grumpy he was and this and that, but you know he had a hard row to hoe. He lost his wife, he lost his house, left with three little girls, no money. Must have been very, very nerve-wracking for him sometimes, you know. But you don't think of this when you're growing up. But I often think of it now. Of course he was very much 'Do as I say and do it now, not a minute from now but NOW!' And you jumped when he spoke and did it. You didn't talk back. You'd get a backhander if you did. He had to be that way to survive. He was a gruff person."

Emery, writing that the cougars were the greatest pets to the girls—the affectionate animals a consolation in their rough, motherless life—concluded: "It is believed to be the first and only time in B.C. and possibly anywhere else, that cougars have been household pets. The girls' father, who has hunted among cougars for 50 years, says the cougar is not a vicious animal. In fact, he claims, all animals are far more inclined toward friendliness than they have been given credit for. Any savagery they might possess is aroused only from fear of being hurt by man or other creatures. Asked if a cougar really screams like a woman as so many stories would have us believe, August Schnarr says: 'No, but they screech and the screech does not resemble a scream. The only other noise a cougar makes is a squeak when it pounces on a deer . . . The cougar is by nature a friendly animal, but also a timid one, and while it may make menacing threats, he seldom carries them out.'

"To Pansy the cougars were the most lovable, cuddlesome and adorable pets she ever had. 'I'd give anything to have another.'"[44]

5

PAPER TRACKS

Schnarr fonds at the Campbell River Museum and Archives.
Judith Williams photo

> All the archived materials are links, discoveries, chance encounters, the visual and acoustic shocks of rooting around amid physical archives. These are the telepathies the bibliomaniacal poet relishes. Rummaging in the archives she finds "a deposit of a future yet to come, gathered and guarded"—you permit yourself liberties—in the first place—happiness.[45]

The Schnarr fonds in the Campbell River Museum contain a treasure trove of papers brought along when August towed his house from Schnarr's Landing to Heriot Bay in the 1950s. Out spill intimate details of the family's life, their employees and contacts, dances and dinners attended, food processed and money paid and received.

I can track where they travelled by boat, how they amused themselves, and that a woman deep in that wilderness wanted a girdle for a twenty-nine-inch waist. Written in pencil at the top of the first page of a black school scribbler is "1927." Under the heading "Woodward's Stores" is "$50 sent with order," a fair sum to be earned trapping or handlogging then. A list of supplies, including "20 lbs salt pork, 2 oz. black pepper" and "1 satin night gown, bust 36 in.," gives a glimpse of Zaida's writing, menus and bedtime apparel. Three gas bills indicate trips south down Lewis Channel between Cortes and West Redonda Islands to the Refuge Cove Store, owned by Jack Tindall and later by the Hope Brothers, who sorted mail, operated as fish buyers and sold fresh meat and produce, boots and clothes. These names, locations and occupations "tell" me the landscape and how people lived in and moved through it.

Pansy, summer 1937, "up Bute."
Pansy Eddington collection

A later school scribbler contains a diary kept by Pansy Schnarr from 1938 into 1939. It begins as August, sixteen-year-old Pansy, fourteen-year-old Pearl and twelve-year-old Marion start building a new gasboat at Owen Bay on Sonora Island and organize moving their houses and sheds onto floats for a permanent move back up Bute.

Why keep a daily record for that period alone? Pansy only mentions attending school twice, and the diary might have been a school assignment to allow her to finish her year. "Dad didn't think girls needed much education," Pansy remembered.[46]

Her diary entries relate date, weather, place, activity and how long it took to travel from A to B. They hint at attendant young men, record a visit of the Fair family—into which Pansy later married—and document the girls' contribution to the family economy. I know more about their daily activities than I do of the lives of my grandparents!

In 1937 August had received a Bear Bay log sale licence. Renewed in August 1940 as Timber Sale Contract X2734 in the Vancouver Forest District, it encompassed 716 acres south along the shore from Bear River to northwest of Melleresh Point in Bute. August could cut 75,000 feet of fir, for $2.50 per 1,000 feet of stumpage; 40,000 feet of cedar; and any hemlock, balsam or other species. He paid $18.25 for timber cruising, $2.00 for the log-marking hammer and $16.25 as 10 per cent of expected stumpage. Zaida's brother Chas. A. Lansell witnessed the contract.

Several gaps with "Can't remember" scrawled across the page allow my imagination to enter Pansy's narrative. I see August in the Owen Bay shed, setting the teeth of his saw after he informed the girls they were moving back up Bute to log. I imagine a feisty Pearl drying supper dishes: Mad!

Marion enters the house with an armload of wood, followed by a cougar. She kneels down to feed the fire, leaves the stove door open a crack so she can see the flames, a forbidden waste of fuel according to August. Sitting, she shifts one leg out toward the heat, raises the other knee and leans back against the settee as the cougar rolls alongside her thigh to encourage a rub. A hand settles into fur.

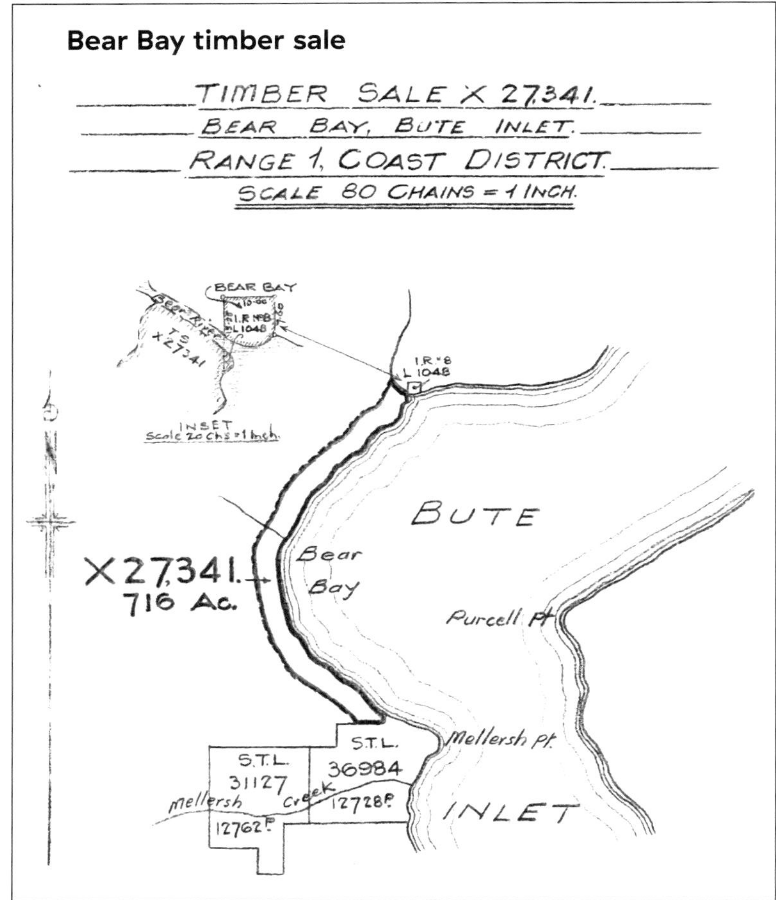

Bear Bay timber sale

Pansy is bent over a table, opening a new school scribbler like the one in which her mother, and now she, records the Woodward's orders, payment to men who log for August, log booms shipped south and boom chains returned. In the top corner of the first page she writes:

> 1938, Jan. 22. Killed pig.[47]
>
> 23rd: Went up to Van der Est's to set four cougar traps after dinner. After we came home, we pulled logs under boathouse.
>
> Jan. 24. We cut pig up this morning. Uncle Charlie came in to ask August for use of a jack. After dinner he worked around in boat shed. Got another log under. It sprinkled pretty near all day. It was very cold. August caulked two bulkheads and stern of his boat. Pulled two more logs under shed. Lent Case two mattocks. Put young pigs in smoke house. Weather mild. Looked at traps but never got anything.

The Schnarrs had begun beefing up their boat shed with new log floatation in preparation for towing their camp up Bute.

On January 26, August went to Blind Channel in a light north wind and bought a keel for the new boat, bilge strakes, a keelson, gas and candy, for a total of $8.07. A far jaunt in an old gasboat of the day, his route was north out of Owen Bay through Gypsy Shoals, west down Okisollo Channel and rapids, north through Discovery Channel past the Walkem Islands and into Mayne Passage to the sizeable cannery and sawmill at Blind Channel. Rumour has it there was a still.

> Jan. 28. Mail day today and Mrs. Van der Est was in, so was Mike. Of course August got nothing done. Mike for dinner, Logan for supper. North wind blowing today. Rather cold. Got settlement for logs.
>
> 29th. Went up to look at traps but had no luck. August never got much work done on boat. North wind blowing.

30th. August brought some lumber over from the mill and put it upstairs to dry. Worked in boatshed. It snowed last night and today. Made settlement with Logan on Southgate supplies: $100. To be received later.

31st. August worked on his rowboat. Snowed a little today . . . Still North wind blowing.

The Okisollo and Hole-in-the-Wall rapids make Owen Bay on Sonora Island one of the most difficult communities to access in Discovery Passage. Loggers settled there in the 1900s and established a school in a settler's house in 1927. Needing more students to keep it open, they advertised for a teacher with children. Alma Van der Est, her husband, Bill, and their six children arrived. Alma and her children rowed across the bay to the school, where wind blew through cracks in the walls, and water flooded the floor during high spring tides. Mt. Van der Est lies between the heads of Phillips and Frederick Arms.

On February 1, Pansy complained, as she did all winter, that August spent the day talking to their neighbour, Schibler, and not working on the new boat. After school the girls had a snowball fight in five inches of snow.

Two days later August and neighbour Mike went cougar hunting at Barnes Bay, where August had killed Leo and Girlie's mother, and then on by boat to Tipton's Store at Surge Narrows. It snowed 12 inches more during that day.

Feb. 4. Got ten little pigs today. Made house for Boliver (the boar). Stopped snowing. Milder.

Feb. 5. August made stove for steam box. Brought his winch and [drag] saw float from the pass as it got loose. It's been raining all day. Tonight it hailed. Blowing South Easter

August and Mike installed the stove and steam box in the boatshed. A boat builder, Mr. Whitfield, arrived on the 11th, and that night they all went to a lively whist dinner. Pansy sent Eaton's store $9.95 for a banjo.

Below left: Marion, Pearl and Pansy with cougar. When you look away, what do you see: the pyramidal grouping, teeth, the chain or snow? *Unknown commercial photographer. Image MCR 15625 courtesy of the Museum at Campbell River*

Below right: Treed cougar. *August Schnarr photo. Image MCR 14437 courtesy of the Museum at Campbell River*

Above: Jean Schibler and Leo.
August Schnarr photo. Cougar Companions *album. Image MCR 2006-8 courtesy of the Museum at Campbell River*

Top right: Biddie Belton, left, is not sure being photographed with a cougar is a good idea.
Unknown commercial photographer. Image MCR 19615 courtesy of the Museum at Campbell River

Lower right: Marion, Pearl, Girlie and Leo, Owen Bay.
Schnarr family photo. Image MCR 2006-8 courtesy of the Museum at Campbell River

Feb. 12. August and Mr. Whitfield worked in the boatshed. They cut out the keel and frame. Made another coil [for steam box] and made it backwards. Snowed pretty near all day.

13th. Yesterday we all went up to Van der Est's for dinner. So, of course, there was nothing done. Snowed all day. Put down 6 inches. North wind.

The essential steam box didn't work. August spent several days trying to fix it. When he finally got it working, they built a rock fireplace and boiled a drum full of water to make steam to bend the planks for the new boat.

On the 19th, Mr. Van der Est came to help Mr. Whitfield put the boat keel on, and August went to Stuart Island on the 26th to ask Uncle Charlie to put some cedar logs in the water so he could build a big float to transport their houses up-inlet. By the 28th the girls had brought a maple bow-stem from the Van der Ests and started planking the boat. On March 1, Pansy wrote that "A. J. Spilsbury came in and August bought a radio from him." This $59.95 radio would facilitate the remote logging show, but Pansy fussed that they were still planking the boat necessary for the up-inlet move to begin logging.

March 5th. Worked around boat. Put another plank on and puttied nail holes. Dance tonight.

6th, Did we have fun!

March 8. Putting the last few planks on. We took pictures of the boat yesterday. Took pictures of us three girls in our dance dresses. We spoiled a whole roll of film. The sun was lovely and warm. Battery on radio is dead.

Raised on Savary Island, north of Powell River, Jim Spilsbury built his first crystal radio set at seventeen. By 1938 he was boating the coast in the *Five B.R.*, selling, installing and maintaining radios for private clients and logging companies. That same year Spilsbury was amazed to be able to install a radio connection from Twin Islands to Kyoto, Japan, via Vancouver. This was in the Twin Islands house Charlie Rasmussen built for Richard Andrews. When the war began, the RCMP instantly ripped out this connection. After World War II, Spilsbury, as well as Jack Tindall, who had owned the Refuge Cove Store, created Queen Charlotte Airlines to move loggers in and out of remote areas, transforming the industry.

"Nice kitty!" "Bur-r-r," replied Leo.

How would you like a mountain lion for a playmate?

By FRANCIS DICKIE

Cougar Pets

ON THE lonely wilderness island of Sonora, off the coast of British Columbia, three girls—Marion, Pearl and Pansy Schnarr—have brought up from babyhood two unique pets.

In January, 1935, their father, August Schnarr, a noted trapper, killed a large female mountain lion or cougar. As he was skinning it he noticed that the animal had recently become a mother. There is a bounty of $20 per head on these destructive animals, which will kill anything from a cat to a cow, so he backtracked through the snow and finally located the den at the foot of a fallen cedar tree. There he found four blind, mewing kittens. He threw them into his packsack and carried them to his cabin.

His three daughters—Marion aged eleven, Pearl twelve, and Pansy fourteen—had been motherless since infancy, and their hearts went out to the helpless kittens. They fed them warm canned milk out of a pop bottle with a baby's nipple fastened on top, and at the end of fourteen days the kittens opened their eyes.

Two of the kittens died, but when summer came, the two surviving mountain lions (which also are known as pumas, cougars, panthers and "painters"), now grown to the size of small dogs, roamed about the yard and even ventured into the forest. But always they returned.

For some eight months this idyllic state of happy kittenhood continued, then one afternoon Marion saw Leo, the larger of the two lions, sneaking toward the corral in which was kept one of the family pigs. Running at full speed, she reached the corral just as Leo did. She sprang between the pig and mountain lion, slapped the latter across the face, seized him by the collar and dragged him away.

Pens were now built for the animals and they were chained to them, but one day Leo broke free and chased a neighbor's goat. Pansy ran after her pet and seized his chain, and the animal became docile in her hands. Later, Leo escaped again and roamed the woods all night, only to return to his friends in the morning.

For two years now, the Schnarr girls have kept the two mountain lions as pets, playing with them as other girls play with house cats, often with an empty tomato can which is used as a sort of football. Yet no stranger dares approach the animals. Occasionally the girls doctor their pets, the latter submitting to treatment with even more docility than the average house cat.

Thus on a lonely island three girls and two ordinarily savage beasts have grown to maturity together—a unique companionship, perhaps the first on record on the North American Continent.

Above: Francis Barrow photo of Jim Spilsbury's *Five B.R.* in Bute Inlet below the "Needles."

Image MCR 20110-19 courtesy of the Museum at Campbell River

Left: *Cougar Companions* album page with Francis Dickie article.

Image MCR 2006-8 courtesy of the Museum at Campbell River

Warmer weather allowed them to putty nail holes for painting. Three days later August took to bed with a hot water bottle on his hip as it was bothering him.

14th. Turned boat over.

On the 15th Pansy noted that the previous night's terrible southeaster had wrecked many things and was still blowing. She did not know that *Maclean's* magazine published "Cougar Pets" by Francis Dickie that day. The article was illustrated with two photos of the girls and cougars in snow, taken by a professional photographer.

***Loggerette* in process, Owen Bay.** *Schnarr family photo. Image MCR 14390 courtesy of the Museum at Campbell River*

The wind picked up at Owen Bay on the 17th, so August cancelled a trip to Stuart Island and went deer hunting. When the wind fell on the 18th he did go to Stuart Island, and Pansy, annoyed he didn't come home until nine on the morning of the 19th, grumbled at another delay.

Margaret (centre) and Jack Parrish (far right) with their children—baby Ron and Roy—and Amy and Francis Barrow, Stuart Island, c. 1936. *Francis Barrow photo. Image MCR 10345 courtesy of the Museum at Campbell River*

Mar. 20. Pearl and Marion went out after dinner to paint the boat. We went up to Van der Est's for supper. Snowed about one inch while we were up there.

22nd. August had Mr. Case over helping him make the shoe for his boat. Mr. Van der Est and Mr. Whitfield building deck.

24th. August took part of his engine over to Parrish's Machine Shop. Us three girls went out and puttied. Mr. Whitfield is still making deck and Mr. Van der Est mixed paint and painted bottom.

Jack Parrish's Stuart Island machine shop was a regular upcoast boat repair stop. The engine Pansy refers to must have been for the new boat. Parrish or blacksmith Case, also on Stuart Island, could have welded the metal tripod that supported the propeller in the airboat, although the first stand was wood. August had money in hand to pay men to build the new boat and repair engines so he could prepare for a more remote life.

Pansy's gnomic March 24 diary entry, "Allan (Game Warden) punched our cougar. Skin (Leo)," is difficult to deconstruct. Leo seems to have died sometime during 1937 or early 1938. Did Game Warden Allan Grenhome "pinch" them for not turning in the nose for bounty? That was illegal. Did he "pinch" the pelt to show off the remains of a hand-raised cougar, a feat never previously accomplished? That the family would keep their pet's pelt may seem gruesome, but not to a trapping family that killed, skinned and butchered animals regularly. Pearl said August conducted an inconclusive post-mortem on Leo to ascertain why he died. Pansy wrote no more about Leo but says that, as the weather improved and the boat neared completion, they framed up a cabin at Owen Bay to stay in once the houses were moved to Bute. August retrieved his engine from Stuart Island and moved what Pansy calls "his boat," the canoe, out of the boatshed so they could lower the new boat into the water. They planed boards for the new cabin and built doorways.

> Mar. 30th. Getting tar ready for decks and front of boat. Cabin nearly finished. Doors and windows to put in yet. Wind is coming from the west still. Weather very warm.
>
> Apr.1, April Fool's Day. Finish tacking canvas on [boat deck]. Mr. Whitfield made hatchway.

After Whitfield finished the hatches, August paid him $265.00 and took him to Stuart Island to catch the steamer. The Schnarrs went to a party and August slept all the next day. On the 5th they put guardrails on the boat and August went to Stuart Island to bring home his new engine.

> April 7th. Us girls went out to boathouse after dinner and puttied and painted part of cabin. The weather was just fair today.
>
> 8th. Mail day. August got the stuff for his boat that Mr. Whitfield sent up. One piece of glass missing.
>
> April 9th. Sent report of cougar down to Allan [Game Warden] to get bounty. The two girls went out to finish what they didn't do on Thursday. After dinner Pearl and I planted Early Rose Potatoes. August still putting engine in boat.
>
> 10th. We went "hooter" hunting today over to Barnes bay. We caught four grouse. Marion shot two of them. Got boom-chains today.
>
> 12th. Worked on boat and engine. After supper we killed the bore [boar] Boliver.

The next day they cut up and salted the pig. On the 14th Pansy put the pig head and other bones and meat on to boil all day while they planted nearly a sack of potatoes in rain. August helped them tie up loganberry plants.

On the 22nd Marion cleaned the shavings and chips out of the inside of the boat and they dug more garden. Next day their teenage friend Frankie Colbard came from Read Island, had supper and stayed the night.

Below left: Pansy, Pearl, Marion and Frank Colbard display a giant Pacific octopus in front of potato hills, Owen Bay, 1938. *Pansy Eddington collection*

Below right: Pansy, August, Marion and Pearl on top of their new gasboat, *Loggerette*. Cougar Companions *album. Image MCR 2006-8 courtesy of the Museum at Campbell River*

After Frank left on April 24, the weather was good enough for the girls to spend the next three days puttying and painting the boat grey with green trim. Then there's a big gap in diary entries. On May 19 Pansy wrote that August had put the house sheds on the float a week earlier, and he and Frank were going down to Surge Narrows to phone for a tug. Uncle Charlie was paid $10.00 for helping move the house.

Although handloggers' floathouses were regularly shifted on and off land up and down the coast to follow new log sales, a successful move required a nice sense of timing in relation to the tides. An extra-high daylight tide, available in May and June, was necessary to winch buildings onto a float, tow them to the new site and haul them back onto land. They could then be jacked up on pilings above the highest tide and levelled. Massive pulleys and winches, a nicely developed expertise and a degree of luck were needed to ease the wooden buildings along and not pull them apart.

August's 1934 loss of his floathouse due to a wind at the mouth of Bute must have been uppermost in his mind. The tow route out of Owen Bay is unnervingly documented in the *Coast Pilot*, which states the course is subject to stiff currents and overfalls along the Upper Rapids that flow into the bay and east through the narrow entrance to Hole-in-the-Wall rapids. I have seen the narrows sport a spectacular five-foot-deep hole in the ocean. Organized movement at slack water was called for. Pansy remained as patiently impatient as possible about the move.

> May 20. Tug came to take the houses up Bute. August isn't home so we wait. August and Frank came home at a quarter to one and we were leaving at one. August, Frank, Pearl and Marion went back to get the cougar in the cage. Got up Bute at 11 PM.

A bill from M.R. Cliff and B.C. Mills Towing Company is dated May 21, 1938, "for a tow of camp from Owen Bay to Bear River, Bute Inlet for the period May 20 at 4 to May 21st at 3,—$50.00."

> May 21. We're up Bute, tied where the boom was last year. After dinner August and Frank towed the buildings down to the slides in the corner. The sun still shines as hot as ever.

The handlogging August practised at Bear Bay was part of a dynamic, almost freebooting, period of BC forestry history. Due to the necessity of steep slopes and sheltered waters for booming and towing, it was mainly a Canadian enterprise. When August first came to the coast, the logger could cruise the shore in a rowboat and just set up shop, but the government soon taxed handlogging licences. Given the terrain, Section 22 of the Forest Act, pertaining to handlogging, reads like a dare: "The holder of a license granted under this section shall not use any machinery propelled other than or operated otherwise than by muscular power to carry out lumbering operations under this license."

The many operations tucked into small bays up the coast could use only an axe, saw, jack, wedge, gravity, ingenuity and a considerable degree of enterprise to send a felled tree shooting downslope into the water to be boomed and towed to mills. If there was a second logger, the two could use a crosscut saw to fell the trees. No logger would fall a bad tree because the picky market wanted clear timber. The aim was to fall a clear tree as close to the beach as possible on a slope providing enough momentum to send it all the way down to the water. Higher up, trees were felled across smaller trees and limbed and barked on the underside to make them run. The down-end butt could be bevelled around so it would not catch. A log dump or chute would be

set up to guide logs into a boom bag made of other logs chained together. If a tree did not run, but hit a stump or rock, steel-tipped peaveys and a jack were brought to bear, and the logger had to be nippy to get out of the way when the log took off again. Opportunities for accidents were endless. The last handlogging licence was given to James Stapleton of Toba Inlet in 1965.

Above left: Bunkhouse move, Bear Bay, 1938. *Pansy Eddington collection*

Above right: Levelled floathouses, Schnarr Camp, 1938. *Pansy Eddington collection*

On May 24, with the house still on its raft, August and Frank began logging while the girls cleared brush for the house site. On the 31st they moved the house over below the site, and on June 1, with the tide high and the persistent inlet swells at ease, they winched the house off the raft. The next day the bunkhouse was moved up on land and levelled. The Swanbergs, whose camp was across the channel, dropped in with mail.

On June 3, August and Frank worked thirteen hours boring holes into boomsticks to hold the chains that would create the boom bag to contain logs. Pansy put Girlie, who'd been wandering free, on a chain.

The Schnarrs now regularly travelled out of Bute on the *Loggerette* for mail and supplies. Pansy is particular about travel times because it was close to 35 miles from the Landing down to the mouth of Bute and along the east side of Stuart Island to Harbott Point, with its government wharf, post office and steamer stop. If the tide was truly slack they could cut through the narrow Arran Rapids between Stuart and the mainland and down to the Big Bay community. However, the Arran Rapids' nine-foot overfall at extreme tide changes was a serious navigational hazard.

On a June 4 trip they headed for Owen Bay about 9:15, stayed in the new Owen Bay cabin, left at 8:30 the next day, hit slack tide at "the Hole" and arrived at Stuart Island about 3:30. On the return, they waited in "the Hole" for the tide and got back to Owen Bay about 8:45. Leaving there at noon the next day in calm, warm weather, they reached Bear Bay at 7:30.

> June 6. August and Frank put the [water] pipeline in and were brushing out for walk. We killed a pig this evening. Weather very warm.

The next day August and Frank put up the walk and porch. Pansy drew her single diary illustration of the outhouse propped up over the water on tree rounds.

Schnarr's hand auger. *Judith Williams photo*

Arran Rapids overfall.
August Schnarr photo. Image MCR 20447-80 courtesy of the Museum at Campbell River

June 8. The wind and swells were pretty rough today. Before dinner the men fixed the anchor and after dinner took a couple of jacks up the hill. They were jacking a log when a sharp boulder squashed August's big toe. So he came home and lay around.

10th. August hasn't gone to work because of his toe. Frank pretty nearly got one [log] to the water. The pig got too close to the cougar pen and the cougar took a chunk out of his ear. Frank came home with his nose bleeding because the jack handle flew up and hit him in the nose.

On June 11, August and two of the girls fixed the boom. Frank went to work, and later August, Marion and Pearl went up the hill to fall some trees that were sent into the chute. On the 15th Pansy towed three trees into the boom.

June 16th. Men went to work. Got one tree in the water in the forenoon. Girls tied it to boom. Afternoon got two logs in. The weather is cloudy today.

17th. This morning August stayed home because of his eye. After dinner he fell a tree. Changed anchorage of gas boat. The sun was fairly warm. Swanbergs came over and borrowed 10 cans of milk.

On the 25th they travelled to Stuart Island for gas and went to Owen Bay, where they had supper and breakfast at the "Vans." Their mail did not turn up on the steamer, but they bought fish and headed home in rough weather. On the 29th, August and Frank got two logs to the water's edge and Pearl painted the table. They picked blackberries but a bear ate August's. Pansy tried to tow trees into the boom but the inlet swell was too great.

July 1. Frank cut his finger. Ten trees altogether today. August and the two girls went down to take trees out of the chute. Frank had to stay home on account of his finger. They got four trees in and fixed boom as one of the lines broke. The weather was nice and warm.

July 4th. Fairs were here for breakfast and took us over to camp to get our order. After dinner Frank came home as his finger bothered him. The sun shone brightly today too. After dinner us three girls went blackberry picking and just before we got to the patch we scared out a bear. Killed pig last night. Charged battery.

Schnarr boom with "riders." Looking south down channel with longboat at bottom right.
August Schnarr photo. Image MCR 20447-12 courtesy of the Museum at Campbell River

5th. Cut pig up this morning. Frank came in at 4 PM this evening with a cut in his head. A rock dropped on it. Just cut the skin. August felled three trees and undercut three more. One came out but split in half. The other one smashed at the bottom. One stuck up above.

July 13. Pulled riders on boom today. Frank lost the stamping hammer over-board. We had a little over half of them stamped.

14th. After dishes and pigs were done, Aug and us three girls went timber cruising. I got stung with a Hornet. August never found any good timber . . . Fired Frank today.

Accident-prone Frank got his boat ready and left. The loss of the stamping hammer was more serious than might be evident. Its mark consisted of a number and one of three letters, *x y* or *z*, and with the hammer the handlogger branded the butt-end of his logs. The incised code told who cut the log, where the log came from, what kind of land it came off and what royalty was due to the Crown. Each log in a boom had to be stamped if the logger were to be paid and fulfill his licence obligations. The Schnarrs had to obtain a new hammer, by mail, before the boom could be sent south and sold.

August now had to fall trees alone. In her album, Pearl identified a "silent partner" set-up he used when cutting down a large tree by himself. In the photo (see page 88) his springboard is cantilevered out from the tree (lower right) so he can stand on it above the root flare. He's made the undercut (at right above the springboard) in the direction the tree is to fall, and strung his limber line, usually a sapling, with a string to the right end of the saw (from the top right and down). The bark is cut away so he can see where he is sawing from another springboard (hidden at left).

"The preferred wood for springboards was strong, light, yellow cedar," August said when he described this falling technique to the crew taping him at the Campbell River Museum. "They would split out the board and taper it down and curve it in here to lighten. A metal shoe went on the end with a lip that stuck in and levered into the tree. The whole thing had a spring to it that helped.

Top: "Silent partner" logging rig set-up.
August Schnarr photo. Image MCR 14432 courtesy of the Museum at Campbell River

Below left: Drawing #1 "Silent partner" logging rig.
Judith Williams illustration

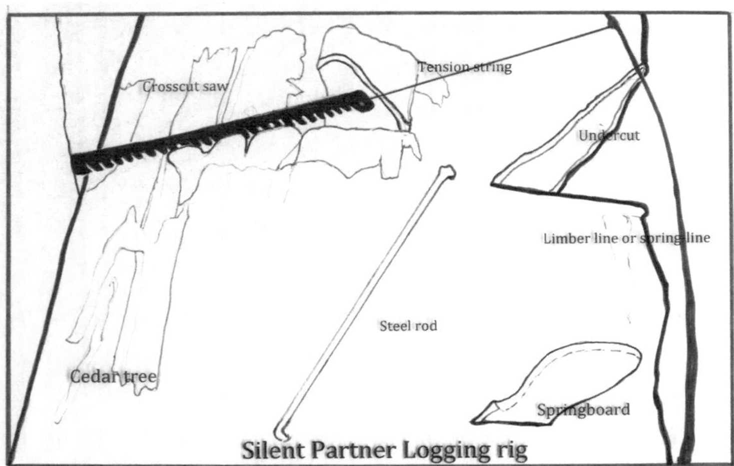

Above right: August with a felled tree, thought to be that shown at the top of this page.
Glen Macklin collection

"I felled all kinds of trees with a spring pole . . . Well, let's say this is the tree here and you're gonna fall it just downhill. You walk straight in [from the water] and then . . . put an undercut in and fall that way [toward the water] . . . Then you put a spring pole, a limber pole, out there in front. And from that pole, you put a string, down to your saw . . . with tension on it to pull [the saw back and] . . . up at the same time, not straight over, 'cause then your saw would go straight down [and] make a cut this way, you see. And then, oh boy, that's hard. You want to keep your cuts straight, like this table. Then it's easy! . . . You'd just keep cutting around, make sure you put your cuts straight. And then this [spring] pole . . . pulls up on your saw . . . And then you keep moving your [spring] pole over as you go in. I'd rather do that myself than have most [any] other person on the other side. All this is my ideas when I was working for myself trying to get stuff accomplished."

About the considerable dangers of handlogging, he said, "Do something reckless, that's what you shouldn't do. I wouldn't be here today I guess if it wasn't for that, and even then I got hurt sometimes. We used jacks in handlogging. I got the Ellingsons; they're a better jack, you see. They got gears in them, you know. You can double your power."

By midsummer 1938 it was hot. On July 21 August worked only half a day. He put the clutch band on the engine and the Schnarrs boated to the head of the inlet.

> 22nd. August fell two trees before dinner. Laid around till 3:30 [then] went back to work. I canned 15 quarts meat.
>
> 24th. After supper we went over to the old place to get some logs and apples. We picked 3 boxes off one tree. Sun very warm.

Above: Swanberg logging camp, 1938.
Pansy Eddington collection

Left: Pansy in Bute Inlet. *Loggerette* at anchor on the left, circa 1938.
Courtesy of Albert Fair

Pansy's "old place" is the Schnarr's Landing homestead with its extensive orchards on the mainland south across from Bear Bay. They slept over in the boatshed, had breakfast on the beach and cleaned a fish they took out of a net they'd set. The girls picked three more boxes of apples while August rolled logs off the beach. Back at Bear Bay he went to work, and the three girls went over to Swanbergs' float camp to get mail.

One evening Pansy notes that Gunner, Alex, Red and the boatman came over from Swanbergs' to look at the cougar. On August 6th the Schnarrs went to Owen Bay and had supper at Mrs. Van der Est's. Next day, after digging some of the potatoes they'd planted at Schiblers', they took the *Loggerette* to Stuart to await the steamer, got their order and left for Bute in the rain. At home they began to make up the boom, with August and the girls boring boomsticks, cutting down another tree, and bucking up and stowing logs.

The Fairs—Bert, "Dad," Omar and Lloyd, 1938.
Pansy Eddington collection

Aug. 12, Aug and girls pulled rider on and tightened up boom. After dinner we went over to our old place to pick berries and apples and get six swifter chains. Got a pail of berries and a couple of boxes of apples.

On the 19th the tug came for this boom and the Fairs arrived for a visit. Next day the Fairs took them, in their *Sally-Bruce*, to the head of the inlet and came back for supper in a typical inlet afternoon wind.

Aug. 21. Canned 26 quarts meat this morn. After dinner we went up to the head in our own boat. Blackford's came up afterwards. Spent night there. Sun shone.

22th. Pretty hard night as we slept on the floor. At noon we came home. Blackford's came out to see cougar. Then they left and I made some supper. Gunner brought mail over and box of chocolates. Weather was warm.

After dinner on August 27 the Schnarrs went to Stuart Island, carrying on the next morning to Owen Bay, where they stayed for a picnic. They got their order at Stuart Island and spent the night afloat at Fawn Bluff. Despite thick smoky air from a forest fire, they made it home on the 29th. August went right out, cut down a tree and sent it down to the water to start another boom of logs.

Aug. 31. Aug fell two trees but only one came in. Three boys came over from camp. Joe Bassett rowed over too. I washed floor and clothes. Weather hazy.

Sept. 1. Aug fell five trees and three came in. Girls towed them down to boom. I washed four blankets. Sprinkled a bit.

2nd. August fell three trees and one came in. I made apple jelly and washed kitchen windows. Thundered and rained today.

On September 3, Marion's birthday, August got the biggest tree on the claim in the water.

Girlie at Bear Bay. *August Schnarr negatives. Image MCR 2006-8 courtesy of the Museum at Campbell River*

The girls took the mail over to the Swanbergs and picked up ten boxes of plums and six of good apples. August filed a saw while the girls canned 66 quarts of plums.

> September 5th. Aug got 3 logs in boom today. We canned 65 qtrs. of plums. Jim Smith brought our mail over. Aug received scaling slip for cedar boom. Also selling prices. It rained. 1938.

Pansy's diary skips a year and starts again on what I believe to be Marion's fifteenth birthday, September 3, 1939. They went to Stuart Island in fog for mail and then to Tipton's, where they got three drums of gas.

On September 4 and 5 Pansy made many more quarts of apple jelly while August fixed a steam donkey she had not mentioned before, a considerable mechanical upgrade from the year before. Marion and August oiled some machinery before dinner, and later Pearl and Marion oiled the pipeline. They split new shakes for house repairs. Her note that "After supper dogs were chasing cougar but never got it" suggests Girlie ran free most of the time.

> Sept. 6. Logan was in for breakfast. We bought 13 fish from him. We got 12 quarts canned, and saved one to eat. Logan was in for dinner. Slept rest of afternoon. 5 PM, Ranger Grenhome came in and brought mail. Washed flour sacks. Cloudy. August's log split.

On September 7, 1939, Logan returned for breakfast with a gift of eleven fish, and the diary ends.

The diary and the time and financial record books tally skills the girls added to the overwhelming range of logging tasks, but I feel Pansy writes everything down and leaves everything out! She never mentions Leo had died. "Girlie pined away after and in two years was gone," Pearl said, and then she herself fled, at fifteen, to Vancouver and then to Winnipeg where, she said, "I married a military man."

There is a stiff 1941 letter in the fonds from Mr. Van der Est to August concerning an ongoing payment dispute regarding his son John, his own 1938 work on the *Loggerette*, and eight days Alma cared for the cougars. This undermines the sense of Owen Bay neighbourliness the diary records. August was a very difficult man.

The Fair brothers say their mother, Pansy, had her first paying job at Shoal Bay, date unspecified, and she worked at the Kelsey Bay laundry during the war. In May 1941, on the Coast Mission boat *Columbia* at Redonda Bay, Pansy married Lloyd Fair, who had come with his family to visit the Schnarrs at Bear Bay in 1938. He later stopped to visit on the way back from trapping up the Southgate, and "that," the family said, "was that!" When their son Glen was born late in 1941 they lived aboard the tiny *Essie T*. Norman was born next, and when Albert came along in 1946, the Fairs moved into the cabin the girls had built at Owen Bay between the schoolhouse and the Schiblers.

Albert says that just after he was born, Pansy was sunbathing down on the dock at Owen Bay with the newborn nearby. There was a small noise and, opening her eyes, she was horrified to see the tentacles of a giant Pacific octopus come up over the float toward the babe. She grabbed Albert and ran. He survived to start logging at twelve in Okisollo Channel with his dad, in specially made small boots.

Gillnet fishboats anchored off Bear Bay, c. 1939. *Pansy Eddington collection*

Pansy enjoyed the Owen Bay social life the move provided. "We loved dances," she said, "local music. Somebody would play the violin, somebody the guitar once a month, and you got

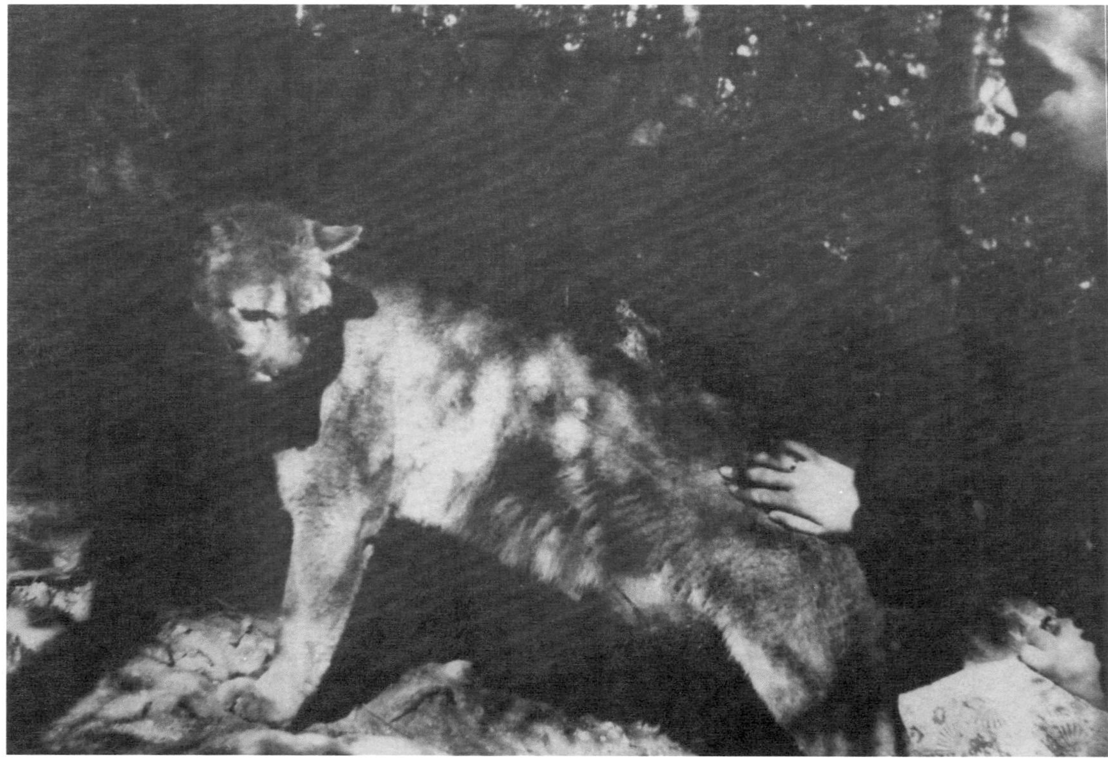

Marion and Girlie, Bear Bay. *August Schnarr negatives. Image MCR 2006-8 courtesy of the Museum at Campbell River*

to know everybody. The loggers, we were loggers. Lloyd, he worked in the bush. Some fishermen would come. It was really nice. I lived right next to the school and I could leave my kids, just run back and see if they were asleep. When we went to Stuart Island we took the kids."

The period of the late 1930s and early 1940s when the girls matured was before the Canadian government passed the Medical Care Act in 1966, and the Schnarrs' medical receipts tell tales. One fonds envelope contains many slips from a Vancouver chiropractor for August, and evidence of an X-ray by the Columbia Coast Mission. August talked tough, but a handlogger gambled his body on his fate and skill.

According to many family members, when Marion was "fourteen," she helped care for the first Mrs. Len Parker while Len trapped. Norman Fair said, "They got to fooling around." Marion became pregnant. In his "resume"[48] Len says his wife "Pearlie died in 1948." Truthfully, official dates and Pansy's diary do not satisfactorily support Marion's rumoured age and condition. A medical bill indicates that on April 3, 1940, "Miss Schnarr had measles" at St. Michael's Hospital, Rock Bay, and returned there April 21. However, birth records indicate Marion had a daughter, named Lennie, on May 29, 1942. She was adopted out. In 1943 Marion was again in the Rock Bay hospital. A bill for $51, dated December 3, 1945, indicates Marion was in St. Vincent's Hospital in Vancouver for fifteen days. There was an additional surgeon's bill for $175.

Cashbooks and tax returns indicate that she continued to log and go up rivers and traplines with August during the '40s. Marion's draft for a letter dated March 12, 1945, indicates they attempted to grow fur by bringing home a group of code-numbered mink from a Vancouver breeder.

> Dear Mr. Hoppe.
>
> Received your letter of the 27th last boat & the bill of sale. We made it out of town O.K. & home in 3 days. All the mink seemed O.K. but two, which were a little slow about eating their food. That was one female and male A.7.1 The trip & handling didn't seem to bother them tho.
>
> Around the first of the month we tried A.7.1. with 3 of the females & he seemed awfully slow. The same day we tried the other male on the other 5 females & he seemed awfully anxious but they did not.
>
> After we put the males back we noticed that one of the females was over on her side kicking. We thought maybe the male had bit her. But she came to again & in a little while appeared allrite. (After being sick to the stomach for a while) . . .
>
> On the seventh we tried them again. Using A.7.1. first. This time he appeared very disinterested. So tried the other male & at the very first cage we put him into he keeled over on his side & took a fit. (Now this male had appeared in very good condition.) So, of course, we took the female out til he came around. Then he was sick for a while & seemed O.K. While we were watching him, the female passed out in the runway and acted much the same, being sick after.
>
> This discouraged us very much & we began to watch them closely. A.7.1. appeared sicker every day until we put him in a small cage and brought him in the house. The first day in the house he looked pretty bad. The second day he looked better & today he really looked well until about 10.00 A.M. Then he took a fit & and one rite after the other for an hour at the end of which he died. We cut him open & and examined him and could find nothing wrong inside at all.
>
> We sure would like some advice on this. They have been fed nothing but codfish & and mostly red cod or snapper. We tried it ground and whole. We have not tried to mate them at all since the 7th.
>
> If there is anything we can do, send a telegram or write & take the letter rite down & put

it on the Union boat. (If it goes in the mail it may not catch the boat.) Hoping you have some solution. Will close, Yours Truly

August was often asked to help search for people lost up the inlet valleys. Another of Marion's draft letters, dated August 3, 1945, firmly states a claim they made after helping the provincial police search for the body of Trygve Iverson, who had left for Twin Lake on July 15, 1945, with two timber cruisers to ascertain the Homathko's utility for floating down pulpwood. The police report states: "It is a treacherous river and he was drowned on July 29th by the upsetting of a raft on which he and his companions Einer Bergan and Erlund Green were floating downriver." Green and Bergan reported the death and returned upriver with the police in the longboat "of August and Marion Schnarr."

"We made four trips up the Homathko R," Marion wrote. "First to meet party coming down. The second after T. Iverson was drowned Aug. 3, Mrs. Iverson paid. Two other trips were made later. Because the river was too high at the time to make a thorough search we waited til later as requested and searched after the river dropped. These trips were exceedingly dangerous and required a special boat and knowledge of the river. I might mention that on the last trip we nearly got caught ourselves.

"We are only working people and had to drop our own work to do the service. As Mrs. Iverson

Log boom at mouth of Homathko River. *Charlie Rasmussen collection*

has paid for two of these trips, we think it is only proper that the Provincial Police should stand for the other two."

Mrs. Iverson paid the Schnarrs $200 for two trips, but the police only ponied up $50 for both of the subsequent two. The body was never found. The active river logging Iverson had been exploring continued until the 1960s, when the first roads were pushed up the valleys.

A notice in the *Owen Bay News* states Marion and Len Parker's son Bert were engaged on November 14, 1946. Both are identified as from Bute Inlet. They married January 31, 1947.

The challenging complexity of Marion's life from 1938 to 1946, combined with Pearl's remark to Glen about being taken advantage of by "those old guys up there," fills me with a fierce, protective rage. I cannot be sure of anything except official records, but I am proud of how these young women worked, coped and grew! Dad was a demanding curmudgeon or worse, and Len Parker is described by more than one observer as a charming, conniving old goat, but the girls were tough. They escaped and became competent, admired adults despite a minimal education and a rough raising.

You sense the determined firming up of Marion's character as you learn of her 1940s life in Bute. Her nephews recall Aunt Marion as a straight speaker, not shying away from correcting them, but also warm and caring. Marion was thoughtful enough to compile the family members' *Cougar Companions* albums, portraying the sisters' unique life with the cougars, and to co-author a book about her controversial uncle, Canadian rumrunner Johnny Schnarr. She and Bert Parker made a life with their three other daughters. Lennie, the daughter born in 1942, tracked her down, claimed Len Parker's First Nations heritage and brought her children to see their grandmother.

I am awed by the girls' extraordinary years with Girlie and Leo, and the hard, physical workdays described in Pansy's diary. Her children treasure the *Cougar Companions* albums and the diary that records an upcoast world they experienced differently, and they are proud of their mother's competence within what they acknowledge was a very demanding life.

INTERLUDE IV
GOLD

Pearl's *Cougar Companions* album contained a print of August's 1926 photograph of Butite Charlie Mould in his cocked fedora and fringed logging boots, propping up a dead grizzly on a float. That's a pretty big bear, and Charlie Mould—well, some folks say he was a pretty big liar.

When I asked Pearl if she remembered the Moulds, she turned and looked out the window. "Ooo-whooowff!—Jackie," she sighed. The girls, of course, knew Charlie and his son, Jack, all their lives. A second photo of Charlie and the grizzly includes a small Pansy at extreme left.

Charlie Mould told evolving tales concerning an Indigenous man he'd once seen kill another to gain a giant gold nugget. He said that man later tracked him for *his* gold, and Charlie may or

Charlie Mould, 21, trapping on the Southgate River, 1926.
August Schnarr photo. Image MCR 20447-43 courtesy of the Museum at Campbell River

may not have killed his tracker to get the giant nugget. The thing about oral history, a wise First Nations chief once told me, is that you can remember differently.

Charlie believed the nugget's source was in Bute, and when son Jack was sixteen, Charlie took him up the inlet to see a wood-framed "Spanish cave" hewn into a mountainside to enlarge its natural size, a wooden door said to be carved with "Spanish helmets," and a hide-lined bucket of a kind used for smelting. There were strange markings on a tree. The Moulds insisted the Spanish had mined and smelted gold in Bute in 1792, and the commanders, somehow informed of the imminent arrival of British ships, scuttled a gold-loaded galleon in Waddington Harbour silt for safekeeping. Maps showing a "Galleon Creek" joining the Teaquahan River north of Southgate Peak may have influenced the Moulds' theories: two of Jack's mining claims lie directly south of that creek.

The tent-shaped rock.[49]

The "Spanish" material, Jack said, was proof of their mining activity and gave credence to a Bute location for a lost gold mine. Well, maybe. But coastal First Nations encased cadavers in cedar boxes, sometimes grooved or engraved, that were hidden in trees, caves or crevices. Carved planks were erected to mark territory and gravesites, and arbourglyphs, faces and signs were carved into live trees. Any worked wooden surface could be of Indigenous origin but, as is usual in treasure stories, all this provocative evidence was buried, according to Jack, in the construction of a Southgate logging road. That Jack couldn't locate Charlie's "evidence" proved a stumbling block when soliciting mine investment.

The foundation of this whole edifice rested on folk tales concerning the Katzie/Nanaimo man Slumach, who appeared in New Westminster during the 1890s with a plentiful supply of gold. He lived it up in bars and cathouses until his funds were gone, then headed out to the bush with a young Indigenous girl and reappeared with more gold the next year. Although rumour placed his gold vein in the Pitt River area, the Moulds were convinced it was in Bute and that Slumach had found the Spanish gold.

Now, Slumach was no sweetheart. The girls he took away never returned, and records show that at 8 a.m. on January 16, 1891, Slumach was hanged at the Royal City Jail for the murder of the "half-breed Louis Bee." His body was claimed by his nephew, the respected Katzie shaman Simon Pierre, and buried within the old jail. On the scaffold, before he died, eighty-year-old Slumach is said to have called out "Nika memloose, mine memloose" (If I am dead, the mine is dead), cursing anyone who dared search for his gold.

Slumach's curse is said to have claimed its first victim after San Francisco miner John Jackson reportedly found the gold. Jackson returned to civilization, and on May 28, 1924, wrote to a

Southgate River cabin painting.
Mike Moore photo

Detail of cabin wall painting, Southgate River, 2011.
Mike Moore photo

friend that his gold cache was buried under a tent-shaped rock facing a creek that came straight out of a mountain, bubbled in places over bedrock bright yellow with gold, and disappeared. This site could be found by lining up three specific peaks. Jackson died two years later without having retrieved his cache.

In 1931, Volcanic Brown, a sprightly eighty-year-old prospector from the Kootenays, acquired a copy of Jackson's letter. Brown never returned from his last trip to the Pitt River area. His body wasn't found, but a jar containing 11 ounces of pure gold was discovered in his last camp.

Jack claimed that during a helicopter reconnaissance he'd found the tent-shaped rock, the bubbling creek and the three peaks near BC archaeology sites EeSf3 and EeSf4, which contained rock shelters with "Spanish remains." The archaeology site reports note male and female human remains, fragments of boxes and scraps of matting consistent with Indigenous burials. Jack's mining claims map, now attached to these particular government archaeology files, situates two "Jackson's Mines" north and south of Southgate Peak near the burials, and four "Slumach's Mines" around Southgate Peak. Jack conflated useful elements of the archaeological information to raise more funds, and he said that in the process of installing a landing stage for renewed surveying, he and his nephew had found the scuttled Spanish galleon. Jack tantalized his lawyer by describing a video he said he had of the ship, sunk in the silt of the Southgate delta. The lawyer complained, "Jack says the underwater video is on its way, but it never arrives."

Raising money to continue exploration was a constant problem, but minute amounts of gold flake, the promised but never delivered underwater video, tales of the misplaced Spanish cave and photographs of the tent-shaped rock were strewn in front of enough prospective investors who could not resist a gamble, and Jack forged on. The green-gold grow-op back in the bush helped.

Twirling a bookstand in the Lund Store one day, I found *Jack Mould and the Curse of Gold* by Elizabeth Hawkins. The book explicated Charlie Mould's conviction that the mine that supplied Slumach with the gold he spent in New Westminster in the 1890s was located in Bute Inlet and had been mined by Spaniards. Over the years the cockeyed logic of Charlie and Jack's gold stories, and local raconteurs' tall tales regarding the misadventures and misdemeanours of the Moulds, *père et fils*, built up a legend about Jack, exploratory dynamiting and gold. Recently, a painting was discovered in the Moulds' old cabin up the Southgate. If you allowed yourself to give the tiniest amount of credence to the Slumach's mine story, the artwork's dated tombstones (for Slumach, second from left; Jackson, third from left; and Brown, fourth) and the scene of men madly digging in a graveyard by lantern light under a spiral-tracked mountain surmounted by a tropic island lunette and ascending bird would have sucked you further along the trail. It was a hoot.

The cabin painting may date from the 1990s, when Jack Mould had attained, both in his own mind and in the minds of some observers, legendary status. Pearl was right to sigh! In and out of jail for things that were always someone else's fault, he surfaced in a variety of local tales. Jack, it is said, was once sitting in a Vancouver bar with a pal, drinking beer, when a third man entered and shot the pal. "Jack," he gasped, "I think I'm dying!" Jack looked him over, remarked, "I believe you are," downed the rest of his beer and left. He was, after all, a busy mining entrepreneur devoting every hour to planting rumours, digging up funding and salting gold claims.

Jack Mould and the Curse of Gold is the lasting result of all these efforts. It contains photos purporting to be this and perhaps that. However, Jack's mention of his heavy use of dynamite in and around his claims attracted my attention when I was compiling *Dynamite Stories*, a book about the enthusiastic use of nitroglycerine in the development of the coastal BC economy.[50] Character-revealing Mould stories popped up unexpectedly. When Bobo and I boated up Bute Inlet in the late 1990s, we'd pass a lopsided grey barge hauled onto the Southgate mud flats. It seemed deserted, but Chuck Burchill, who'd taken over running the Homathko River logging camp up the other river, assured us it was occupied by Jack Mould. Relations between the two men were tense, as Chuck had heard Jack dynamiting the Homalco Band's burial area at Potato Point, at the mouth of the Homathko east of X̲we'malhkwu Reserve, and called the RCMP. Jack claimed Chuck was poisoning him.

Detail of cabin wall painting, Southgate River, 2011.
Mike Moore photo

Chuck once drove us beyond the Teaquahan River to see the marbled murrelet nests in old-growth hemlock. On the way back he picked up two hikers who'd set off six days earlier on a walk into the Interior along the rumoured Homalco grease trail. When supplies and enthusiasm ran short they turned back, taking a shortcut across the tidal flats below Mould's barge. Jack emerged, shotgun cocked, and demanded they get off his property or he'd set an unseen dog on them. "Normal behaviour," Chuck laughed, "should anyone seek to disturb Jack's ruminations."

After I included a censorious note about Jack's generous deployment of explosives at Potato Point in *Dynamite Stories* in 2003, his dossier dropped into deep storage, but a writer's discourtesies have a way of coming back to haunt her. Near the end of August 2007, I was standing on the Refuge Cove Store porch on West Redonda Island, idly watching a floatplane dock. Out hopped the pilot, two shirtless young toughs sucking on their beers, and a burly, bearded older man in scruffy shorts leading a small canine, perhaps a Peekapoo, on a pink leash. They strolled up the dock into the store and the bearded man disappeared into the back. I joined Lucy Robertson, who was behind the till, as he reappeared brandishing a copy of *Jack Mould and the Curse of Gold.*

"They've got my book," he crowed. "The one I wrote!" He waved the paperback energetically in front of the pilot. "It's my book, the one I told you about. Got to buy a copy."

"Surely you get them from the publisher," the pilot said.

Jack turned on him. "*That* bastard! No, gotta get this for a friend."

I sidled up to Lucy and whispered, "Don't say my name!"

Of course I wanted to talk to the legendary Jack Mould, but I most emphatically did not want to be known as the person who'd written about him in a critical way. He was a man widely rumoured to sue or shoot those who crossed him, although I did not think the attendant dog was going to be the kind of threat he'd indicated to the hikers it could be.

"So where you off to?" I tendered as an opener.

"Ah! Nowhere. Just taking the boys out," said Jack, who, at the end of the pink leash, looked rather like an untidy teddy bear. "They've been working hard surveying for me up Bute. Thought I'd come for the ride."

With my tongue firmly in my cheek, I asked, "So, what's your book about?"

"Yeah! I wrote that, all about my search for gold. Don't know—I just have to find it. I wanted the gold all my life and I want the glory."

After years of hearing stories about Jack, now, looking at his aging face, the slumped belly, the Peekapoo—for heaven's sake! I realized all I really knew about Jack Mould came from the accounts of others. The Peekapoo was disorienting.

Three weeks later, Lucy called my attention to an item in the September 12 *Campbell River Mirror.* A week after Jack had been at Refuge, a member of a hiking party had been severely injured during a rock slide, and a rescue party arrived in Bute. A Jack Mould was helpful. The hiker's body was retrieved and removed. A week later a timber survey crew flew in and found Jack's truck by the river. Its doors were open and a large number of water containers lay around. A pair of shoes were found downriver, one in the water and the other high and dry on the bank. The Peekapoo, curled up inside the cab, was pretty happy to see anyone. Jack was nowhere to be found.

Two weeks on, the same paper reported that J&S Kulta Mining of Nanaimo had applied for a permit to explore for gold. President Sulo Poystila said, "Senior members of the company have been prospecting in the area for 50 years." He requested permission to put exploration teams in Bute at an existing base camp at the head of the inlet across Waddington Harbour from Hamilton Point: the location of Jack's barge.

What was going on? Hikers came in. One was hurt and everyone, including Jack, swung into action to rescue him. Jack disappeared. The police arrived to question Chuck closely and demanded a list of loggers and visitors at Homathko Camp during the relevant time frame. The Homalco complained they had not been consulted and the fishing lodges decried the effect of mining operations on salmon spawning, but finding seventy-one-year-old Jack did not seem to be anybody's top priority. In the old days it would have been August, the territory expert, hired to search, but bodies ending up in upcoast waters are seldom found.

6

ʔANAQOX TSEN GWAIADTEN: TRAIL TOWARD BUTE INLET

What routes did August and the girls follow up the Homathko and Southgate Rivers to the Interior? Pansy's confirmation of her dad's winter trips up to Chilko Lake, Charlie Rasmussen's diary of the 1929 trip and the Moulds' belief in Slumach's route down from the Interior all suggest it's useful to shuffle August's inland photo images with those in Knewstubb's hydro survey report to see where they correspond and indicate plausible routes up both valleys to the Chilcotin.

Head of Franklyn Arm, south end of Chilko Lake, c. 1929.
"Water Power Investigations: Report on Taseko–Chilko–Homatho project," page 1637, photo 41[51]

Due to the topographically controlling terrain, every usable route inevitably intersects with and overlaps sites and trails used for millennia by the Homalco and Tŝilhqot'in Peoples. It seems obvious August's route to Chilko Lake would make use of established Indigenous trails when useful. It is revealing to position First Nation place names, images and activities within economically purposeful non-Indigenous usages to indicate how concepts of territory, ownership and exploitation shifted as the incoming Walkers, Moulds, Schnarrs and hydro surveyors or logging companies competed for inlet resources.

Before contact, the Homalco (X̱we'malhkwu), a member of the Coast Salish group that included the Klahoose and Sliammon tribes, spoke Éy7á7juuthem, a dialect of the Mainland

Village of the Friendly Indians, Bute Inlet **engraving based on an original ink-and-wash drawing made by Thomas Heddington, July 1792.**
Judith Williams photo

Chilko Lake, Chilcotin drainage and Indigenous trails to tidewater.
Source: BC Parks, Ts'il?os Provincial Park Master Plan

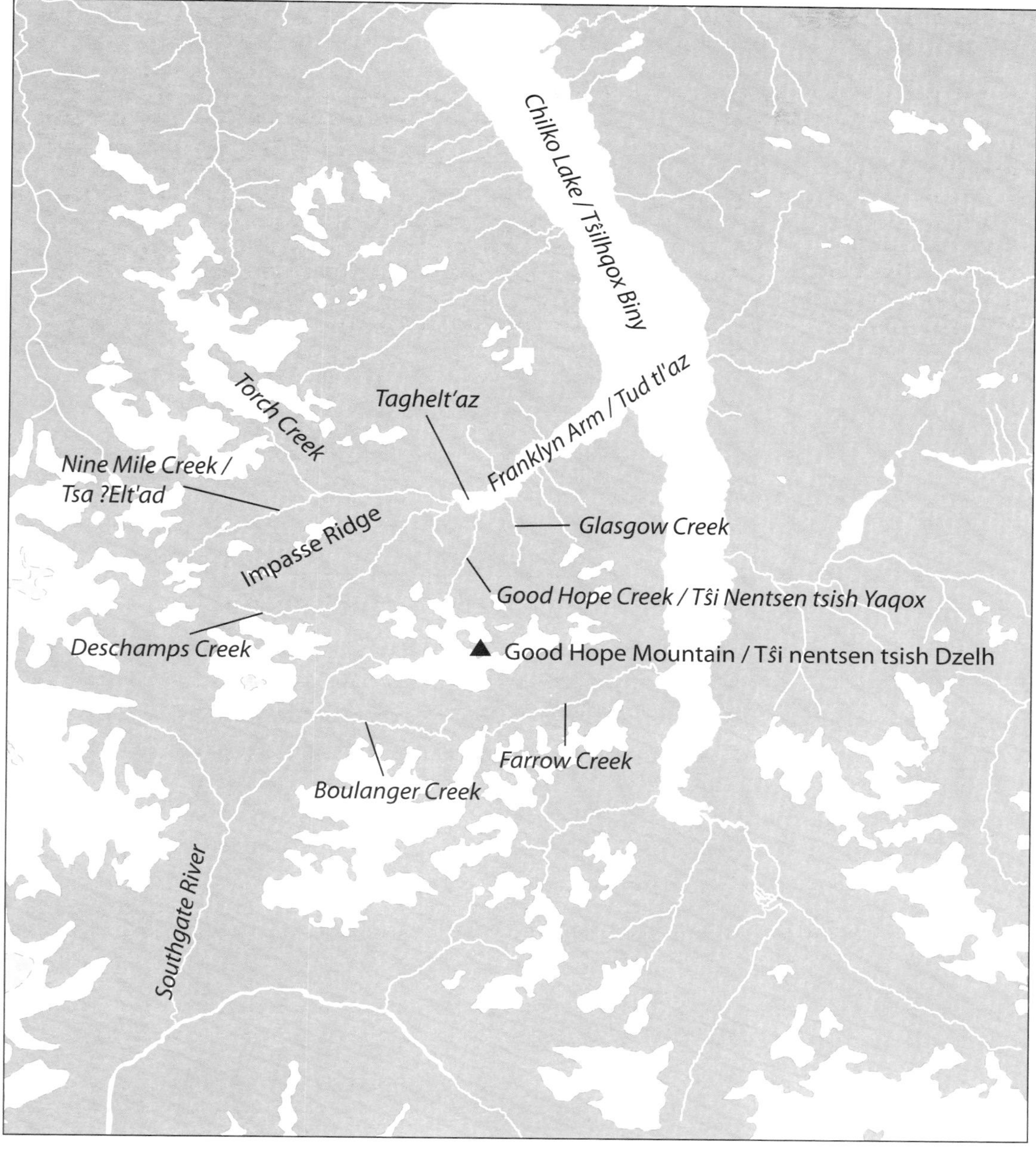

Comox language. The Homalco wintered in their Bute Inlet territory, where all species of salmon ran up the rivers to spawn in feeder creeks. Subgroups went to sites at the Miimaya River and Pi7pk̲nech at Orford Bay, and seasonally to Saayuick Village on the mainland west of the Arran Rapids. Some Homalco owned Tatapoose village and fort in White Rock Pass, between Read and Maurelle Islands, where the east pass entrance is marked by a First Nations pictograph panel. From Tatapoose, people could move north through Surge Narrows Rapids to Waiatt Bay on Quadra, still ringed by Aboriginal-built clam gardens that have been cultivated for millennia to increase production of butter clams.[52] There are few clam beds in any of the inlets due to the lack of beaches, and the people necessarily travelled out of the inlet seasonally for shellfish. Anthropologist Homer Barnett states that the Homathko Valley underground houses, built by the Homalco above the canyon, were occupied by Tŝilhqot'in People when Robert Homfray sheltered there during his 1861 survey for Waddington, and they indicate a regularly used valley.

"The Lookout," a Homalco fishing site at the junction of the mouth of Bute Inlet and the Arran Rapids, was drawn by Thomas Heddington in July 1792 during the British exploration of the Inside Passage and engraved for Vancouver's *A Voyage of Discovery to the North Pacific Ocean, and Round the World* as "Village of the Friendly Indians." In his journal, botanist Archibald Menzies recorded that where James Johnstone's survey crew had first seen smoke,

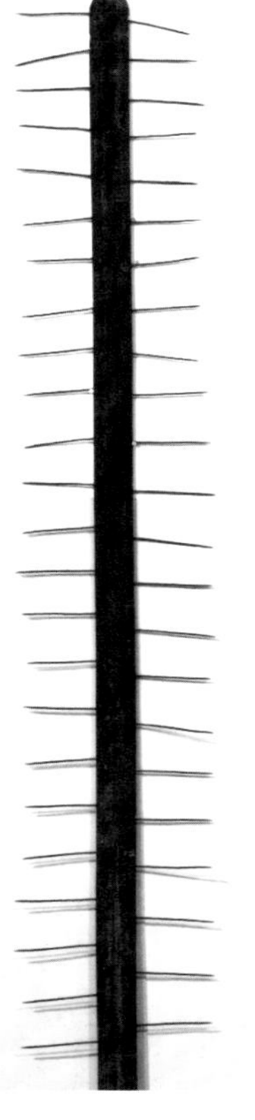

The fishing described by the Spanish was done with the kind of 10-foot rake August made for himself, substituting wire for the bone spikes. *Judith Williams photo*

> they now discovered a pretty considerable village upwards of twenty houses and about thirty canoes laying before it: from which they concluded that its Inhabitants could not be far short of a hundred & fifty. In passing this Village they purchased from the natives a large supply of fresh Herrings for Nails & immediately after entered a narrow Channel leading to the Westward, through which the water rushed in Whirlpools with such rapidity that it was found extremely difficult even to track the Boats along the shore against it, & this could hardly be accomplished had it not been for the friendly activity of the Natives who in the most voluntary manner afforded them every assistance.

Captains Galiano and Valdes encountered this fishing station at the same time and added a parallel set of Spanish names for the same territory to their maps.

> They saw a large settlement situated in the pleasant plain on the west point of the mouth of the channel of Quintano [Bute Inlet] and proceeded to coast along to the mouth of Angostura [Arran Rapids]. In the neighbourhood there were a large number of canoes with two or three Indians in each, engaged in sardine fishing. The instrument they used in this task was a rounded piece of wood some three yards long, one third of which was studded with hooks. In this way, dropping this kind of wide toothed comb into the sea, making various draws with it, they caught the sardines on its hooks and gathered them into the canoes. Many of the natives approached our officers without showing the least nervousness.[53]

Using their arms to indicate the arc of the sun, the Homalco fishermen made an effort to tell the Spanish the correct time to pass the Stuart Island rapids (regularly finessed by the Schnarrs). Misunderstanding, the Spanish captains allowed their 46-foot goletas to be caught in tidal whirlpools that turned them around so often that their text states it was the most terrifying portion of the entire trip. They named the passage Angostura de Los Commandants in memory of the captains' understandable agitation.

Ever curious, August sought evidence of Indigenous sites and Waddington's road-building activities as he moved from his Bear Bay and Schnarr's Landing homes upriver to trap. Initial information about the violent conflict that followed the road-building intrusion into this territory was written up by English artist/alpinist Frederick Whymper and published with his engraved paintings in the 1875 *Illustrated London News*. Whymper arrived by boat at Waddington's Homathko Camp on March 22, 1864, a month before the Tŝilhqot'in attack on the road crew, to make "views" of the grand landscape. One of his watercolours places two First Nations people in a canoe on the Homathko River opposite a traditional Indigenous house and two post-contact-style buildings at Indian Reserve (IR) #2A, below the start of the road and the present Homathko Camp.

***Homathko River Facing Upstream*, watercolour by Frederick Whymper, 1864.**
Image PDP00109 courtesy of the Royal BC Museum and Archives

Whymper hired Tŝilhqot'in Chief Tellot to guide him up the zigzag pass above the canyon to sketch glaciated areas where Charlie and August later trapped. "On reaching the glacier," Whymper wrote,

Whymper's engraving of the Homathko River cable-ferry crossing, based on a drawing made in March 1864, before the killing of the ferryman. The Tŝilhqot'in warriors cut the ferry loose to hinder pursuit, and it was swept downstream.

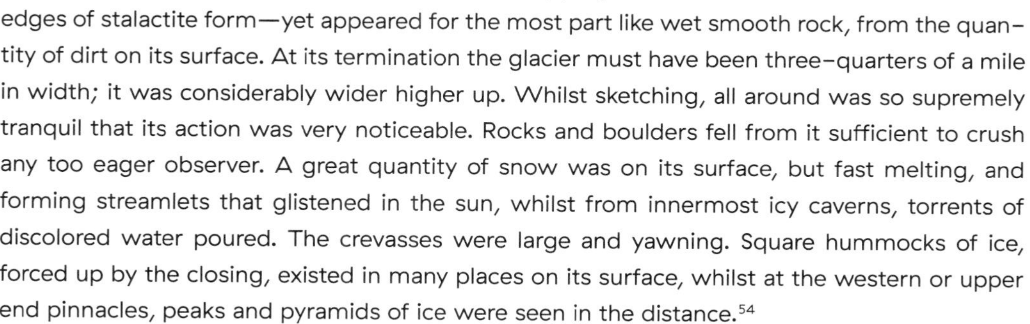

> its presence was rendered very obvious, by the cracking of the ice and the careening of the stones from its surface. This was incessant; now a shower of pebbles, now a few hundred weight of boulders, and now a thimbleful of sand, but always something coming over. The ice—very evidently such at the cracks where you saw its true colour and its dripping lower edges of stalactite form—yet appeared for the most part like wet smooth rock, from the quantity of dirt on its surface. At its termination the glacier must have been three-quarters of a mile in width; it was considerably wider higher up. Whilst sketching, all around was so supremely tranquil that its action was very noticeable. Rocks and boulders fell from it sufficient to crush any too eager observer. A great quantity of snow was on its surface, but fast melting, and forming streamlets that glistened in the sun, whilst from innermost icy caverns, torrents of discolored water poured. The crevasses were large and yawning. Square hummocks of ice, forced up by the closing, existed in many places on its surface, whilst at the western or upper end pinnacles, peaks and pyramids of ice were seen in the distance.[54]

Descending the valley, Whymper stopped briefly at the road builder's ferry station with "S," the man in charge, then continued down the trail with the pack train to the road crew station at the mouth of the river. The next morning, friendly First Nations packers broke into his room and excitedly reported that "S" had been murdered by the Tŝilhqot'in for refusing to give away his provisions and property.

Dismissing the story, Whymper set off with other men down-inlet in a canoe owned by a

During an 1870s Bute survey Charles Horetzky took a photo of two Homalco men with a canoe 12 miles from the mouth of the Homathko River, as well as an evocative image of the tight Homathko Canyon over which Whymper and later August travelled.

Charles Horetzky photos, Vancouver Public Library 8542 and 8543

"Clayoosh Indian," a hard taskmaster who had them paddle to Victoria in five days. On May 12, 1864, the artist was horrified to hear the ferryman had indeed been killed the morning the Indians had tried to warn him, and fourteen road workers were killed the following day.

Members of the Tŝilhqot'in tribe that had been terribly afflicted by the 1860s smallpox epidemic had come to pack for Waddington's road. They were threatened with more smallpox by a road boss who came from Victoria, and were then implicated in the deaths of the road crew.

Over the years, Whymper's story was combined with the Victoria *Colonist*'s reports of the duplicitous capture of the Tŝilhqot'in warriors who claimed to have declared war, accounts of a trial in which the men were found guilty of murder and condemned to be hanged, and an eyewitness tale from Qwittie, the Homalco man who survived the killings, to produce oral versions of these unique BC events. These stories fired the interest of August and many others to search, as I did in the 1990s, for any evidence that brought that history and landscape alive.[55] On Monday, March 26, 2018, Canadian prime minister Justin Trudeau exonerated the six Tŝilhqot'in chiefs who were hanged for murder after being invited to parlay with the British colonial authorities who had invaded their territory.

The Tŝilhqot'in Band, the southernmost of the Athapaskan ethnic groups, occupied the Chilcotin drainage, above Homalco territory, with two major concentrations near Chilko Lake. (Chilko Lake's Tŝilhqot'in name, Tŝilhqox Biny, means "Tŝilhqot'in People's lake," suggesting they specifically claim it as their own and not Homalco territory.) These interfacing tribes are known to have had intertribal conflicts, and in 1990 Klahoose elders and sisters Elizabeth Harry and Susan Pielle said the Tŝilhqot'in had occasionally captured and married Homalco and Klahoose women.

The BC government's enthusiastic encouragement of explorers, settlers, entrepreneurs and developers to do as they wished with the inlet areas caused the abandonment of many Homalco and Tŝilhqot'in sites. When the McKenna–McBride Commission was establishing "Indian

Church House. *Image MCR 19779 courtesy of the Museum at Campbell River*

reserves" in the Bute area in 1914, they identified Muushkin, a Homalco village on Sonora Island, as IR #5a, even though the people had already moved across to Church House (U7p), IR #6, at the inlet's mouth on the mainland, after a severe "Bute" flattened Muushkin in 1896. Although the Homalco seldom spent extended periods of time at the old inlet sites, they still lived and fished at the head of the inlet in the 1890s and worked for settlers. Pansy and Pearl spoke of trading with them into the 1940s. The Homalco Band now runs its "Bears of Bute" camp at Pi'7k̲nech at the Orford River.

The Homathko townsite laid out by the Royal Engineers on the north side of the river mouth was abandoned after Waddington died in 1872. Waddington had been in Ottawa, promoting his plans for a transcontinental railway with a terminus at the head of Bute Inlet, when he died of

***Waddington's Homathko Canyon Road*, drawing by Frederick Whymper, 1864.**
Image PDP00105 courtesy of the Royal BC Museum and Archives

Blasting and metal pins for Waddington's cantilevered Homathko Canyon road.
August Schnarr photo. Image MCR 6698 courtesy of the Museum at Campbell River

smallpox. Remaining settlers on both sides of the inlet head were so desperate the government had to finance their removal, and their buildings stood for many years as a reminder of the collapse of the high hopes Waddington had twice inspired. By the 1920s the Southgate Logging Company was established at the mouth of the Southgate where early Bute settlers lived, and an era of raw resource extraction began.

The 1928–30 survey of hydro power potential within these traditional territories the Schnarrs moved through indicated the largely glacier-fed Homathko River, with its wide seasonal variations in runoff, would not in itself be a reliable source of power. However, Chief Engineer Knewstubb thought a diversion, via tunnels, of a balanced flow from Taseko and Chilko Lakes, which drain into the Fraser River, to storage in Tatlayoko Lake, at the headwaters of the Homathko, would overcome this problem. His report included maps of the proposed dam, spillway, storage and tunnel routes, and plotted a water intake, dam and tunnel from Franklyn Arm at the west side of Chilko.

Knewstubb stated that salmon ran into Chilko Lake, but since none spawned above Homathko Canyon, where they planned a dam for water tunnelled from Chilko, he implied there would be no impact on spawning. However, salmon spawned in all the rivers and creeks feeding into the Homathko below the canyon. Then and now, any road building or logging in the inlet creates landslides and silting detrimental to spawners, and silt moving downstream affects young fish as they exit. After years of logging, Bute runs are now much reduced.

The hydro report included photographs of the remains of Waddington's wagon road within the survey area, including a Schnarr photo depicting the blasted-out rock bench, denuded of any structure. A Whymper watercolour depicts the same section of Homathko Canyon prior to the killing of the road crew.

Regarding a possible road from Chilko Lake via Franklyn Pass to the Southgate River for his proposed tunnel, Knewstubb wrote, "There is a fair trail from the head of Franklin Arm to

The hydro report includes a photo of what Knewstubb refers to, in the racist vernacular of the time, as a "Siwash" crossing of the Southgate River. A companion picture has a man straddling that kind of log bridge over the river. Examination with a magnifying glass suggests the figure is August in his usual long underwear, suspenders and hat, hanging over the chasm on the crossing log. He is seated at the centre of a wonderful three-dimensional star created by the log, an oblique rock fissure and the log-cast shadow emerging from a cavern that, on closer examination, is more a product of a slant of light or trick of the mind than a cavity.

the Southgate Crossing, 4–5 miles below Boulanger Cabin which can be used by horses, and a rough trail continues to the (Southgate) Forks. It is recorded somewhere that cattle or horses have been driven over this . . . old Indian route [to Bute. And] in the lake region . . . it is quite feasible to drive a team and wagon . . . to Nemaiah Valley."

He said a powerhouse might be built either at a First Nations crossing on the upper Southgate or up the Bishop River, which an old map marks as "Klattsassine's hunting grounds."[56] Knewstubb wrote that it was desirable to have a road connecting the several working points and portals of a tunnel. However, the principal difficulty in the case of a Chilko Pass tunnel would be crossing the Chilko Glacier. He said it was quite easy to traverse on foot for about two months of the year on a gentle grade.[57] He cited two crossings to or from Chilko Lake that August would have known and described to him. The first was "by way of Bishop River to the [Southgate] Forks, then over Franklin Pass to Franklin Arm to a second [route], via the low-pass . . . much used by the Indians in the good old oolachan grease days." The second was "by way of Bishop, Southgate Rivers and [the] Boulanger—'Y' Creek valleys." He said the latter would involve shorter water transport and possibly a lower elevation of pass but with a glaciered summit. He noted a lower pass across the range on the south side of Mt. Chilko.

Regarding the Franklyn Pass route, Knewstubb wrote: "From the head of Franklin Arm [extending west about three-quarters of the distance down Chilko Lake] via Deschamps Creek there is a trail route over the Coast Range and down the Southgate River to Bute Inlet. The summit of this trail is 5700 feet high and is clear of glaciers though snow often lies at the summit till well into summer. From Franklin Arm head a flat swampy valley extends several miles westward, in fact to very near the summit [of the pass]."

Knewstubb noted that this route connected to a grade point west of Boulanger Creek, and to the bank of the upper Southgate, one mile above "Burnt Cabin." Below this cabin the Southgate flows through a box canyon and down to a point just above the "Siwash" crossing at the Forks with the Bishop River.

Over the years August would have made use of all the routes and cabins mentioned in the report, and Knewstubb's "much used . . . in the good old oolachan grease days" track would be of considerable interest, as it was said Indigenous people could come down this trail from Chilko Lake in eight days. August laid out traplines around the south end of the lake after packing supplies up in stages to cabins, one known as Twenty-One Mile, and another 25 miles from

Crossing the Chilko Glacier. Looking down the head of Chilko Creek Valley. *"Water Power Investigations: Report on Taseko–Chilko–Homatho project," page 1581, photo 27*[58]

"Siwash" crossing, Southgate River Forks. *"Water Power Investigations: Report on Taseko–Chilko–Homatho project," page 1024*[59]

tidewater. The second cabin is the one Johnny Schnarr says they built for the winter during the brothers' 1911–12 explorations when it was cold enough for "mush-ice" to flow in the river.[60]

In 1960, Mount Knewstubb, northwest of Deschamps Creek, was officially named after the chief hydraulic engineer, but the Tŝilhqot'in name, Yanats'idush, meaning "people freeze while on trail over mountain," suggests that peak should be avoided. August and Charlie Rasmussen set marten traps on Tiedemann Glacier in the winter of 1929, so August may have used glaciers for trapping that the Tŝilhqot'in and surveyors viewed as impediments.

In her research of the 1912 circumnavigation of Chilko Lake by the Indigenous guide Kese and the Seattle dentist and alpinist Malcolm Goddard, writer Heather Kellerhals-Stewart found a reference to a white man taking a number of horses over an unspecified route to Bute. She and her husband, engineer Rolf Kellerhals, investigated possible grease trails south from their cabin near Franklyn Arm on Chilko. Heather discovered a Tŝilhqot'in name, ?Anaqox tsen Gwaiadten or "trail toward Bute Inlet," in "Translations for Tŝilhqot'in Features," a section of the *Ts'il?os Provincial Park Master Plan*, compiled when the present park around the lake was established. That trail is located near the headwaters of Deschamps Creek where it flows into Franklyn Arm, the only ice-free route connecting Chilko to Bute.[61]

A lower route beginning at the head of Farrow Creek necessitated crossing a glacier between Boulanger and Farrrow Creeks, whose Tŝilhqot'in name, Tsi nentsen tsish Dzelh, refers to "bad mountain you cannot walk on."[62]

Vern Logan, a descendant of the pioneering Walker family, told me of a grease trail via Wolf Creek near his family's land on the north side of the Southgate, some 24 miles from the river mouth. Dennis and Ray Walker's fourteen-year-old sister Daisy insisted on being a member of the party that trekked up that trail to Chilko to bring down horses, making her the first non-Indigenous woman to go up and down the trail. The horses were driven to swim the river at certain points, and all but one perished. That poor animal, in a dispute about its ownership, was shot.

Pearl said Marion and her dad tended August's daunting Southgate trapline to Chilko Lake together into the 1930s and 1940s. When I asked Marion, she said, "Oh! She [Pearl] did too. She doesn't remember." Whew—what tough young women!

Charlie Mould, hunting for gold and trapping marten when August photographed him at the Southgate in 1926, may not have shared all he knew of these inland routes, but August knew Charlie was searching out a trail Slumach would have had to follow from New Westminster to the Interior and to the gold mine Mould convinced himself was in Bute. If, and it's a big *if*, Slumach came into the Southgate area in the 1890s, he would have walked the ancient web of Indigenous trails that August used and Knewstubb considered.

Although Charlie, Len Parker and Jack Mould staked mining claims all over the inlet from the 1920s into 2000, August was considered the territory expert, guiding, exploring and trapping until the 1970s. Studying a photo from that time, August said it was taken when another surveying party came in to make a map of Mt. Superb. He took the group 1,700 feet up to camp and next day took them up on the glacier. He said that, while waiting for the surveyors, "We two built a cairn, there were a lot of big rocks—built [it] nine feet high and my name is in, put a bottle in [the rocks]."

Glen Macklin climbed up to the cairn and found a jar indicating it was built during that

1970s survey. Did Jack Mould conveniently mistake August's cairn for the "tented rock," one of Jackson's three signs for lining up the fabled gold mine?

Carl Larson says the Southgate route inland is a bigger trek than the Homathko trail that August considered the easier way into the Interior. During his hands-on research of the old routes, Carl was told that August not only had a route up to Chilko, but that men came down that way from the Interior to work at a logging camp 26 miles up, where the Bishop River forks off. Schnarr's Owen Bay neighbour Jack Schibler had a trapper's cabin there into the 1950s. On one of Carl's expeditions, he and Andy Alsager were helicoptered up above the forks, convinced they could raft down. "The water was rough," Carl said, "and I tipped the raft, putting us in the water. But then we drifted down for four wonderful days, down from Bishop junction."

7

GREASE, WAX AND WATER

SOMETIMES, TO CONNECT, YOU HAVE TO STRAIN TO GET THINGS LINKED IN WAYS BEYOND THE NORM AND HOW EACH DOES THAT EXHIBITS WHO WE ARE.

—ANNE CARSON

Grease

What were the "good old oolachan grease days" Knewstubb cites in relation to the Southgate/Chilcotin routes he investigated with August? Oolachan, or eulachon (*Thaleichthys pacifics*), are a small fish, a kind of smelt, that provided an oil much favoured by First Nations for binding dried fish or berry cakes and as a condiment into which a variety of foods were dipped. The fish appeared in early spring when other food sources were depleted.

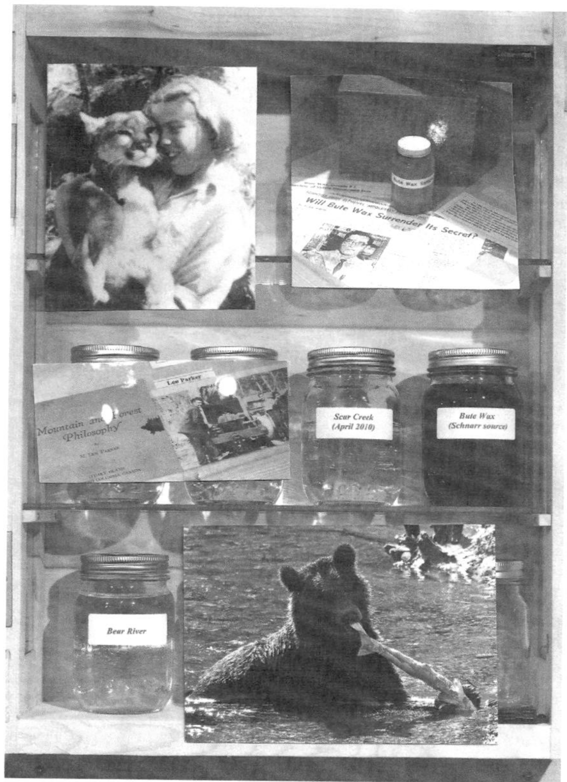

Left: Collaged Bute elements: Pearl and Girlie, Bute wax and water samples, photo of Len Parker, grizzly bear and salmon.
Judith Williams photo

Top right: Eulachon. "This is the most important one—Salmon there are many kind. This one is only one kind." —Chief William Glendale, 1999.
Judith Williams photo

Lower right: Making eulachon oil at Tsawadi in Knight Inlet, 1970s.
Peter McNair photo

Known as T'leena in the Kwakwalla language, eulachon grease was employed as a salve for burns, insect bites, abrasions and chronic skin conditions. It was said to soften leather, was an excellent waterproofing agent and was traditionally used with moss to help seal cracks in canoes and leaky roofs. Along with salmon, sardine, shad and anchovy, eulachon are recognized as a major source of necessary omega-3 oils.[63] Eulachon must be considered a cultural keystone species for Northwest Coast Indigenous people and is valued for its multiple uses and for the cultural bonding activities of grease manufacture, consumption and trade.[64]

August first observed the eulachon fishery, and the processing technique used wherever they ran up coastal rivers, at Tsawadi Village in Knight Inlet sometime between 1910 and 1916. Eulachon were caught in nets as they swam upstream to spawn. Piled in wooden boxes to ripen for ten to fourteen days, the fish were then transferred to watertight boxes filled with water brought to a near boil by the addition of fire-heated rocks.

When a precise temperature was reached and the fish broken up, the oil rose to the surface, was skimmed off, filtered and, pre-contact, stored in bull-kelp bulbs in bentwood boxes. A highly valued commodity throughout the entire territory, it was carried to trade with Interior tribes along paths called "grease trails." The late-run salmon dried and smoked for the winter were low fat, and without the grease's nutrients it would have been more difficult for coastal people to survive the winter on dried salmon, berries and very small amounts of plants. Although the fish once constituted 12 per cent of British Columbia's annual fish economy, their insignificant economic value in the present cash system provided little incentive to preserve them, and many runs of this wonder food are now depleted. They are still harvested by Indigenous people at

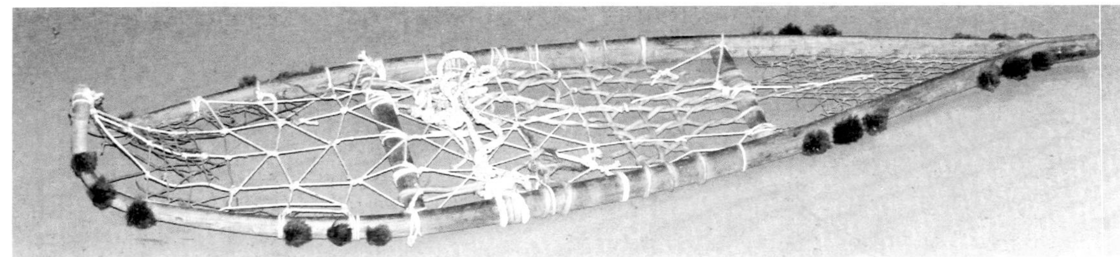

Homalco snowshoe.
Judith Williams photo

Kingcome and Knight Inlets and up the Nass River, where T'leena is used as a food and condiment, and the fish are smoked. A "grease feast," such as that held by Chief William Glendale of Knight Inlet in 2005, where 200 gallons of oil were given away to mark the rebuilding of his grandfather's Big House at Tsatsisnukwomi, remains a high-status event within the contemporary potlatch system.

In the 1930s, Klahoose Chief Julian told anthropologist Homer Barnett that "the Homalco people used to catch eulachons in Bute Inlet, rendering them for the highly prized eulachon grease," but eight years before Barnett's study of the region, a certain man defied the prescriptions applicable to a widower by catching and cooking these fish the day after his wife died. The eulachon promptly disappeared, with a few returning in 1935.[65]

In Kingcome Inlet a designated regulator of the harvest placed a stick in the river, allowing spawning fish to pass. Only when the stick was removed were people allowed to net and prepare the fish for the famously smelly process of making T'leena. In 2015 Dzawada'enuxw elder Geo Dawson was thrilled to report that eulachon surprised Gwai Yi villagers by running so consistently up the Kingcome River for two spring weeks that the river was black with fish. "Never that many before in my life," he said. "We made grease again!"

There are scattered hints of the Homalco trading grease and smoked salmon to the Interior and returning with baskets, berries, animal furs and snowshoes from the Lillooet People. The Tŝilhqot'in came down to fish the Southgate and, as attested by Robert Homfray's 1861 survey story, occasionally moved into Homalco underground houses to smoke-dry fish for winter. Rare materials, like obsidian for micro-blades, could be carried along the ancient web of trade trails south from as far away as the Bella Coola Valley to be exchanged for grease from coastal people.

In the 1990s the Holmalco Band planned to work with an archaeologist to map their grease trail up the Southgate, and the present chief wants to open the trail for trekking. In recent negotiations with the Tŝilhqot'in, who wished to have access to the lower Homathko due to the events of the 1860s, the Homalco learned some of their people had moved up the grease trail, of interest to August and Knewstubb, to live at Chilko Lake for a number of years.

Long-time Homalco researchers Randy Bouchard and Dorothy Kennedy state they never found information about the quality of eulachon oil formerly obtained/processed at the head of Bute Inlet and had not seen ethnographic or ethno-historic records of the Homalco People trading eulachon oil. But in the late 1970s/early 1980s they recorded Homalco elders Ambrose Wilson and Tommy Paul saying that each year in March the Homalco went to Galleon Creek, which empties into the lower portion of the Teaquahan River, to catch spawning eulachon they both smoke-dried and rendered into oil. According to Bouchard's informants, the Homalco name for Galleon Creek does not refer to the presence of eulachon but to the occurrence of the

August in his longboat. Drawing from photo for Maud Emery article. Daily Colonist, *October 2, 1960*

red ochre pigment *thuulhminm*. Wilson and Paul said the Bute eulachon run "failed" around 1900 but also said that eulachons were running there again around 1980. Some Homalco reported the fish around the Southgate River mouth and north of Fawn Bluff in 1995.[66]

Young eulachon depend chiefly on copepods (tiny crustaceans found in salt and fresh water) for food. Since eulachon are said to be fatter in glacier-fed rivers like the Nass, it may be that eulachon in some rivers are less worth processing due to scanty output. Most Bute streams *are* glacier-fed, so why only Galleon Creek below Bute Glacier is used by eulachon is a mystery.[67]

Wax

Bute wax, Schnarr collection. *Judith Williams photo*

Many creatures, including fin whales, sardines, and young smelt, as well as eulachon, eat copepods. This has led me to speculate that eulachon oil and the Bute wax unique to Bute Inlet might share properties derived from these tiny marine creatures, whose bodies are 70 per cent lipid, a fatty, waxy or oily compound that doesn't dissolve in water.

My consideration that the two substances might be chemically related is a by-product of research on the 1860s events on Waddington's road, when references to Bute wax just kept turning up. My citation of M.Y. Williams's paper "Bute Inlet Wax" in *High Slack* brought Sylvia Rasmussen Ives to me with Charlie Rasumussen's wax sample and diary. Williams's paper emphasized that no one had reported the wax's occurrence elsewhere on the coast except at the mouth of Toba Inlet (Yekwamen). He wrote that an astounding mass of the material was said to have appeared in the winter of 1949/50 when freezing conditions held for *five weeks*. Two men living in Bute said that as the cold and wind increased, the water became full of small flakes of the substance. When thrown together and rolled in the waves, it formed into chunks and balls, which grew larger as the weather became colder. The wax-like material was cast against the shore, forming piles as high as six to eight feet. It came *from* the inlet, not into it. Yet when the Homathko and Southgate Rivers were checked, no sign of the substance could be found. No wax was seen until Purcell Point, 19 kilometres (12 miles) south from the head of the inlet, directly across from Bear Bay and northwest of Schnarr's Landing.

The Butites Williams cited, hopeful of finding the wax source, had explored the valley and

Article on Dr. Tikam Jain's analysis of Bute wax, Victoria *Colonist*, December 21, 1968.

SCIENTIST FINDS ELEMENTS 'ABSOLUTELY FASCINATING'

Will Bute Wax Surrender Its Secret?

Times Dec.21,1968 p.12

By ALAN WHITE

One of the mysteries in Dr. Tikam Jain's laboratory at the University of Victoria is a waxlike substance found floating in the waters of Bute Inlet.

He is asking: what is it, where does it come from, has it a use?

Down along the line of scientific investigation, medicine comes upon the scene. But first the wax.

Bute wax — as Dr. Jain has dubbed it — is not in evidence during most of the year. But when waters in the inlet, about 120 miles northwest of Vancouver, fall below 50 degrees, the wax congeals and appears on the surface in tons.

It has not been reported from any other area along the west coast.

LONG STREAKS

Stories told by homesteaders and carried to Dr. Jain tell of the greyish coating being driven in long streaks down the 40-mile inlet ahead of winter winds.

Prospector Frank Lehman, of 1317 Cook St., heard some of these stories and observed the substance "15 or 20 years ago."

It was Mr. Lehman who brought the wax to Dr. Jain's attention.

Engaged in a life-long search for strange chemicals of nature, Mr. Lehman has summarized all the folk-tales about Bute wax.

He has heard a dozen descriptions and explanations in his travels around the inlet.

"There was a lot of talk about it being fish oil — whale oil — or pine oil," he said.

"It is generally a grey color, but there are stories of it being in blues and greens."

"After listening to all the stories, I suggested it might be petroleum in the making — a residual from old, prehistoric oil structures," Mr. Lehman said.

The petroleum theory was only one of several attempts at an explanation.

He also considers it might come from "some bacteria or some sea plant native to that area."

"We know that some bacteria produce wax.

"People up there (Bute Inlet) usually call it Bute Oil. One old-timer had 15 drums of 45-gallon size of it saved up.

FROM WHALES

"One theory they had was that it came from whales who went into the inlet to die.

"Another was that it was some plant peculiar to the area, or pine — but there are none that aren't found in other areas too.

"I have heard a story that the wax is found in one of the fiords of Sweden," Mr. Lehman said. "It may be found in other inlets but not in the same quantity, so it isn't noticed."

'BEFORE MY TIME'

The wax may be a useful substance — and it may not. But discovering its origin and value is part of the fascination of science.

Mr. Lehman said it is one of the things nagging him for an explanation that must come "before my time is up."

Re-enter Dr. Jain ... the chemist—who studied at Agra, India and specializes in plants and waxes derived from them. He wants to break the mysterious substance apart to find out what it is too.

While explaining his work he darts back and forth between his desk and a chalkboard, naming and spelling out chemical elements.

"The origin of its elements are not known," he said recently. "But our chemical investigation will eventually give an answer."

ONE OF 45

He and assistants Robert Striha and Gregory Owen have separated and identified one which makes up about 1 per cent of the wax—called in scientific terms "norditerpene hydrocarbon."

This is the element, only one of 45 in the wax, which may prove the key.

The hydrocarbon has been found in shark livers and in raw petroleum. And Dr. Jain has manufactured it from chlorophyll, found in plants.

"It's a very complex problem," he said. "The 45 constituents in it are absolutely fascinating."

The fascination involves another aspect and brings into consideration medicine—which may or may not be another calculated wild guess about Bute wax.

USED AS SALVE

"I have been told by people in Bute Inlet areas it is used as folk medicine," Dr. Jain said. "Apparently they use it as a salve.

"We don't know what for, or if it works, but we want to find out."

The medical angle explains much of the research under way with Dr. Jain's direction.

JAR IN HANDS of Dr. Tikam Jain, University of Victoria chemist, holds substance which may be animal, vegetable or mineral in origin, or all three. No one knows what wax or jelly-like compound found in waters of Bute Inlet is yet, but extended chemical analysis at Uvic labs may determine the answers to questions being asked.

the shores of the entire inlet. They staked a number of mineral claims, inadvertently discovered Aboriginal archaeology sites, and hired dowser Munday McCrae to survey and make a map of possible wax source sites. They sent samples to various government departments, who said it might be "whale oil" from dead whales, but the locals maintained that whales seldom came up Bute, and the inlet current quickly carried any floating object down-inlet, not up. In the end the analysts acknowledged it was not whale oil but an unknown form of wax ester.

I was struck by a solitary newspaper clipping in the BC Archives files showing Dr. Tikam Jain holding a jar of opaque liquid under the heading "Will Bute Wax Surrender Its Secret?" Jain's wax sample—from "an old timer up Bute who had fifteen 45 gallon drums of the stuff"—was brought to him by prospector Frank Lehman of Victoria. Lehman reported a thick greyish, or occasionally blue or green, coating was sometimes driven down Bute Inlet ahead of winter winds. It might, Lehman thought, be petroleum in the making, residue from old prehistoric oil structures, or produced from some bacteria or sea plant native to that area. Jain, a University of Victoria chemist specializing in plants and the waxes derived from them, said the substance resembled nothing in the known world. He separated and identified one element, 1 per cent of the wax, called *norditerpene hydrocarbon,* which is found in shark livers and in raw petroleum. Jain had manufactured this compound in the lab from chlorophyll found in plants. However, there were forty-four other constituents to the wax.[68]

What was this stuff?

The wax Jain held, like Sylvia Ives's sample, came from August's Bear Bay neighbour Len Parker. Len had recorded the wax's appearance in the winter of 1922, December 1935, January 1936, February 1950, March 1951, November 1955, and during the period of February 14, 1956 to March 1956. He said that in some years he could collect 15 gallons of the substance from 100 yards of beach. Late in May 1951, large, smelly slicks of lodgepole pine pollen were observed in the inlet, and this, along with the golden colour of some wax samples, led to the proposal the substance was pollen based.

In February 1959 the wind again blew with great violence for ten days down the Homathko Valley, from the great icefields surrounding Mt. Waddington in the northeast into Bute Inlet. The temperature dropped nearly to zero, and when the wind suddenly turned to the south, long slicks of Bute wax floated down the inlet and washed up against Len Parker's log boom at Bear River. The wax, collecting around floating debris in the upper three feet of the surface water, created the sixteen-inch balls that rolled against the steep shores at Purcell Point opposite. When the temperature moderated, the balls melted and the material disappeared.[69]

Scientists visited Bute during the summer of 1961 aboard the naval research vessels *Cedarwood* and *Elko* and discovered the inlet bottom was almost entirely of glacial origin and contained only minute amounts of organic material like pollen. No submerged Bute wax was recorded. When samples of Bute wax, all from Len Parker, were analyzed, the scientists concluded the material consisted of esters of fatty acids and fatty alcohols. The material solidified at about 11 degrees Celsius. At the time of testing it was said to be a liquid wax of vegetable origin and from zero to three hundred years old. It is important to note that no scientist was ever in Bute when the wax appeared.

Refusing to be discouraged by the scientists' refusal to declare the wax a petroleum product, Len and August continued experimenting. They washed their hands in it and found it to be powerful cleansing agent. As a paint remover it was unequalled. Despite this, it had a soothing effect on the skin. Used as a waterproofing agent, it rather overdid the soak-in effect and penetrated right into their socks. As a fire starter it blazed up like kerosene. Logging jacks were lubricated, and greased poles seemed Teflon coated. You could burn it as a light, and although its only failure was said to be as oil for engines due to the wax component gumming up the works, Glen Fair mentioned August using it half cut with gas.

Charlie Rasmussen pestered the Department of Mines and Petroleum Resources about the wax well into the 1970s, and stories about its spectacular periodic appearances and useful properties lingered among old-timers. Doris and Norman Hope ran the store at Refuge Cove on West Redonda Island during the '40s and '60s, and the surrounding folk came there by boat for gas and mail arriving on the Union Steamship. Doris recalled August Schnarr boating in one day with a gift of newspaper-wrapped Bute wax that he said was an excellent linoleum floor cleaner. Forgotten temporarily in the warmth of the living room, the substance melted into the rug, and the very fine oil was absorbed by the socks of visiting loggers who were only allowed inside once they removed their caulk boots.

When, sometime later, Doris denied ever having told me the story about Schnarr, I began to think of Bute wax as elusive as memory, unbiddable but emerging under particular conditions. The inlets, not strictly coast and not totally Interior, are a liminal threshold where I felt anything

Think Gum.
Judith Williams photo

could happen. I saw Bute Inlet holding, like a glacier formed long ago, mysteries that a seismic shift, temperature inversion or the right question could release. Getting a look at the wax in situ, however, entailed being in Bute just when I did not want to be there. From late fall until March the wind was predictably unpredictable. Even the first summer we boated south through Bear Bay, the locus of the wax ball episodes, the sea threw up internally lit, jade standing waves, making a passage south like boating over translucent boulders. We had to turn back up-inlet.

Writing in *The Unknown Mountain* about their 1926 attempts to climb Mt. Waddington, Don Munday said, "Adventure can be very much an attitude of mind." I have had exhilarating boat journeys up the grand Knight and Bute Inlets, but tracking down someone to analyze Sylvia's wax sample became an equally stimulating voyage as I was passed along through a sequence of chatty university and government offices across the continent.

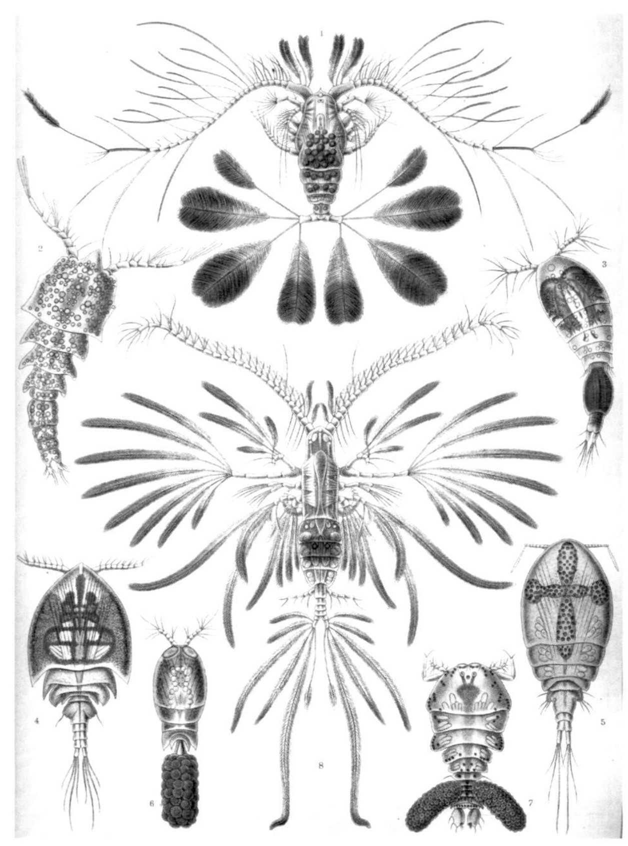

Copepoda, drawing by Ernst Haeckel.
Judith Williams photo

I first called Dr. Michael Healey of the Institute for Resources and Environment at the University of British Columbia. He thought he'd heard of Bute wax but sent me to Steve Calvert, a geochemist in oceanography. Calvert passed me on to Ronald Anderson, a chemist/oceanographer who had been to Bute on a scientific expedition in 1970 and had collected the substance from Len Parker. Although he claimed to have had a wonderful time and been as fascinated as everyone was, Anderson denied expertise and told me to call Andrew Benson at the Scripps Institute of Oceanography in La Jolla, California, who would reveal all.

Dr. Benson speedily returned my call. "Oh no! I am not the real expert," he said but confirmed that the scientific party had concluded Len Parker's substance was derived from copepods. It was a natural wax and oil based on the substance copepods accumulate in a sac in their bodies and use as a metabolic substance in the winter after their food source dwindles. He said at some date, perhaps as long as a hundred years ago, there may have been both a huge bloom of copepods and a sudden die-off. The copepod corpses would accumulate at the bottom of the inlet, where bacteria and time caused the wax sacs to become a more saturated lipid (that is, more oily). Benson told me the brain was mostly composed of lipid. He had produced a few of these lipids in the lab and was amused that one he'd made was being used in a new chewing gum, "Think Gum," that was promoted as a "brain-booster." He was skeptical. Hearing that I was a painter, Benson suggested that since the wax was so stable it would be a perfect artist's medium.

Benson suggested I phone Judd Nevenzel in Los Angeles, who had also been on the Bute trip.

"Nevenzel is an exceptional lipid specialist, although the greatest expert was Bob Bachman in Halifax. We're all friends," he said.

Nevenzel was cranky at first because I pronounced his name incorrectly, but he warmed to the subject and asked if I'd read the article in the San Diego paper. "It's an interview with Andy [Benson] after they had heard about our trip," Judd said. "Andy gave much false information as he'd not actually been on the trip. He insulted this woman. Thing was, he said a woman in Bute used Bute wax as a beauty aid, and even though she was fifty, she looked thirty. Trouble was, she was thirty."

Judd had been doing work in Canada for some time, and in the early 1970s had a chance to visit Bute for research. He and Richard Lee did the collecting and analysis and wrote up their findings for the *Journal of the Fisheries Research Board of Canada.*[70]

"The bodies of copepods are 70 percent lipid," Judd said, "and they bloom in all the inlets, but Bute blooms are thought to be extreme. After a massive die-off, the copepods fall to the bottom of the inlet, and I think the wax that makes up so much of their bodies goes through a natural process of refinement."

Judd thought Richard Lee had taken specimens of live copepods in the spring and fall of 1970–71, but the scientists, who were never in Bute in the winter, received their samples of the wax from Len Parker. They never saw the tree stump that Len and Charlie Rasmussen said acted as a wick to the material's onshore source near Bear Bay, and never saw the wax balls.

Judd said his sample was a naturally refined version of lipid from copepods, specifically *Calanus plumcharus.* Just how the lipid became the waxy substance he could not say, and where the wax was stored when not appearing in the inlet he did not know. Richard Lee proposed that a freshwater deluge from the Bear River, after a sudden thaw melts snow in the mountains, might kill copepods on the water's surface, and their transformation into lipid might be swift. Vast slicks of lipid containing copepod skeletal material have been found in the North Pacific, although no such debris was found in Bute. The mystery of the storage of Bute wax during warm weather, when it is never seen, is perhaps as great as that of its origin. Due to its extreme weather, snowmelts can occur at any time in Bute.

Nevenzel was currently engaged on behalf of Andrew Benson in the analysis of two distinct specimens of eulachon. One was from a river where Indigenous people make T'leena and another from a river where they do not make grease. He was very interested in this analysis because the substance he had found in the fish is a hydrocarbon that survives both the fermentation process and heat and distillation, which he implied were special attributes.

Eulachon oil, like Bute wax, was claimed to have special properties, and certainly the grease's extensive Indigenous use indicates more than mere gustatory necessity and pleasure. To give away hundreds of gallons of grease at a potlatch established the giver as a very high-ranking person indeed. To pour it on the fire so the Big House roof burst into flames was to announce that you and your extended family were the richest and most powerful of all.

I see Bute wax located at a point where environmental reality and narrative overlap to become myth. In many First Nations origin stories, what may seem to be a fanciful narrative turns around to face the observer, "telling" or performing the landscape as the social group's founding site. The "law" of the landscape structure and usage creates the group's social structure. Bute wax is the kind of matter, solid and liquid, hidden and visible, I began looking for in the 1990s to explain to myself the coastal landscape and its processes. Its very un-knowability expresses, perhaps claims, the landscape. It manifests the inexplicable duality of nature in the same way that August's photos of glaciers and waterways, of animals dead and alive, do.

And the wax, with its unknown source, storage and sudden appearance, can act as a key to the memory theatre.

One time, Glen Fair suddenly held his hands out 16 inches apart, saying, "You could grab the wax balls when they were cold, lift them into the boat. August had 45-gallon barrels of it. When Helen and I lived south of Church House we would see chunks of it attached to bits of wood floating out. It would hit on the end of Stuart Island where it was easy to gather. Bute wax fragments were also seen in Basset Bay in Hole-in-Wall, the passage to Owen Bay.

"They always wondered where it came from. There were occasions when the entire inlet would be covered with pollen, so that seemed a possibility. Scientists dragged the bottom but never found a thing. The weather is never now so cold. There was a time August had to carry an axe to chop ice that formed on the canoe from spray, just crossing over to Parker's."

"I saw blobs of the wax once at Surge [Narrows]," Norm Fair said. "It was bitterly cold. I was just a boy."

Water

Eulachon grease was vital to the Indigenous diet. August and Len found Bute wax invaluable. But the nutrient-laden fresh water that rivers, creeks and magnificent thousand-foot waterfalls deliver from the Coast Range glaciers to the inlet are essential, the mother of the fish, grease, wax and much more.

"The 1928–1930 Water Power Investigation of the Taseko–Chilcotin–Homathko" report from the hydro survey August guided was shelved. Another in the 1950s went nowhere, but in

Water sample collection by Judith Williams, Southgate River mouth, August 2010.
Courtesy of Susan Schelle/Mark Gomes

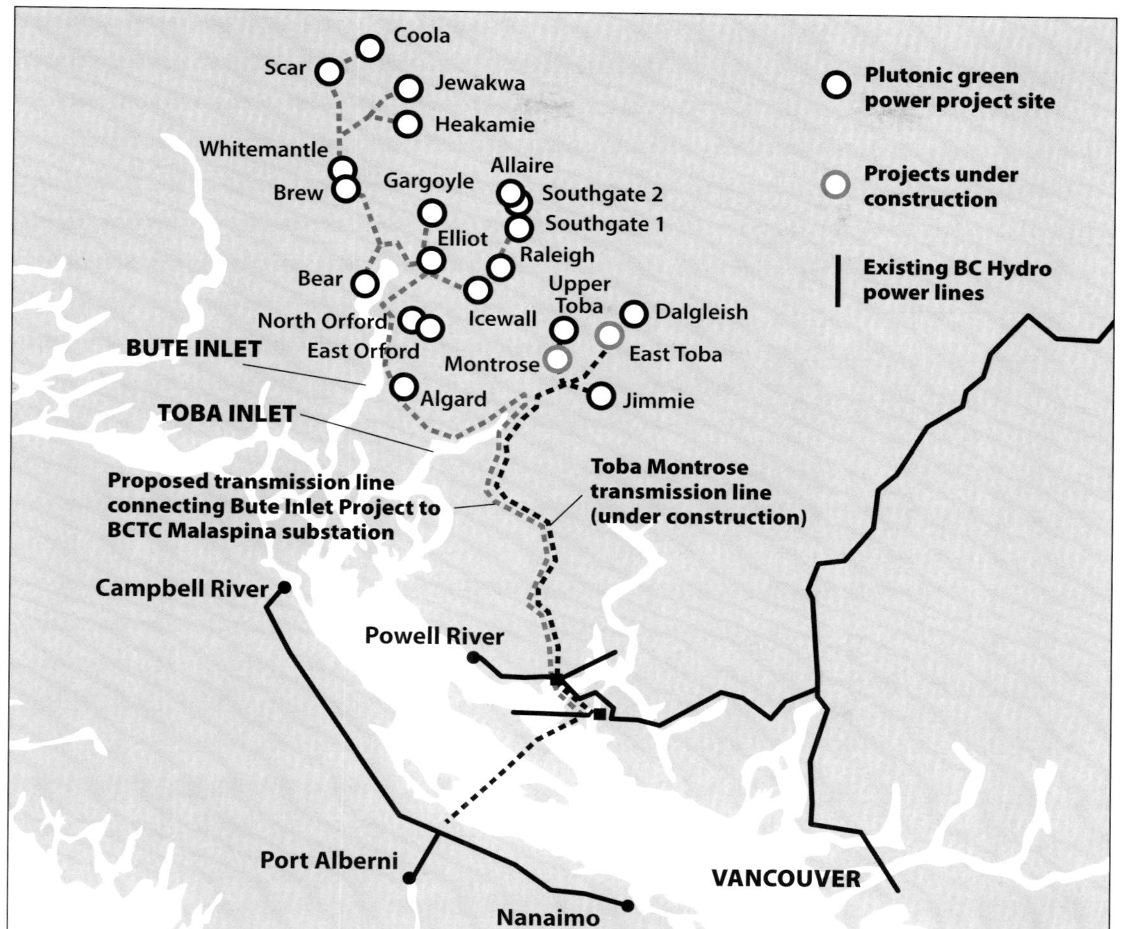

Location of proposed Plutonic/Alterra Bute Inlet run-of-river hydro project sites.
Source: Vancouver Sun, *December 6, 2008*

2008 the Plutonic Power Corporation (which became Alterra and was acquired by Innergex of Quebec in 2018) made eighteen applications to the BC government for run-of-river (ROR) hydro projects in Bute Inlet in another bid to create power from inlet waterways. So-called green power from ROR projects is produced by removing water from large creeks and running it through power stations to create energy. It is then cooled and returned to the watercourse. Plutonic/Alterra was already at work in Toba Inlet and wanted to connect power from the two inlets to run south.

Although small, local, well-sited ROR projects, like that supplying power to Homathko Camp, can be built with minimal impact on the landscape, the process of setting up bigger projects creates extensive environmental degradation. The Bute proposal would have three clusters of ROR projects with an overwhelming seventeen river diversions sending over 90 kilometres (55 miles) of streams and rivers into tunnels and pipelines, and require 443 kilometres (275 miles) of new transmission line, 267 kilometres (165 miles) of permanent roads, and 142 bridges. As Knewstubb noted in the 1930s, there is no natural place to store water, and without storage the flow—and the energy production—would be seasonal.

The potential destruction of fish and animal habitat by construction of multiple dams and power lines alarmed many who treasured the inlet's dramatic wilderness and solitude. But the small Homalco Band felt the project would bring jobs and funds to restore salmon runs affected by 120 years of clearing and logging.[71] The band accepted a fee to allow Plutonic/Alterra's initial territory access. At the same time, the government received a rash of applications for water-bottling licences on many creeks descending down the inlet shores.

If all these projects come to pass, what is unique to the inlet waterways will change, and much of the water resources and land access will come under the control of private commercial interests for long periods of time. The commons is being closed off precisely when it is obvious water is a resource in worldwide demand and the storage glaciers are melting in a moderating coastal climate. The disruption of a grand water resource, to be given into the hands of a private and, at that time, partially foreign-owned company, or put in the plastic bottles we know to be environmentally destructive, solely for corporate profit, appeared to be a stunningly short-sighted use of our shared environmental capital.

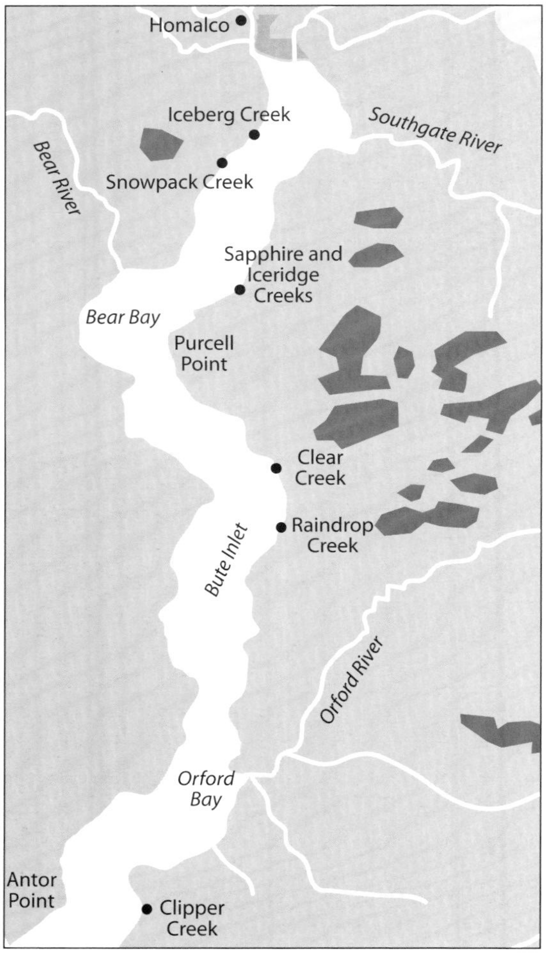

Potential creek bed disruption and damage caused by erosion and silting from ROR dam building prompted the territory's inhabitants and recreational users to create a "Friends of Bute Inlet" website, where they pointed out the difficulties faced in Bute's extreme environment. Clearing the necessary 120-metre-wide (400 feet) corridor down to bedrock along the east side of Bute's precipitous shore so Alterra could run power lines connecting with their Toba output seemed specifically designed to encourage the avalanche-prone inlet to slide more of the landscape into the water.

Arne Liseth, who'd lived at Skookum Point Logging Camp, three-quarters of the way up Bute's east shore, added an instructive story to the website concerning a 1981 Halloween party. The camp's "backyard" was 7,785-foot Mt. Rodney, sheer from peak to saltchuck. Alterra's power line was projected to run along the side of this mountain.

Applications for water extraction allocation in Bute Inlet under the Land and Water Act. *Source:* Campbell River Courier, *December 8, 2010*

October that year had unseasonably heavy snow, but by October 28, a thermal inversion caused air at the top of Mt. Rodney to be warmer than that below. On Halloween Eve, people from many miles around were arriving, and the pre-party started with dinner and drinks and more drinks. Suddenly loud slides were heard a mile or so away from the logging camp, and the tide was observed to go out lower than ever before in a remarkably short time. The smell of sulphur filled the air. Arne and his brother moved their tug to deeper water on the north side of the inlet, but returned it to their dock when the tide appeared to have stabilized. Despite continued rumblings, everyone retired for the night.

About 7:30 the next morning, people at the camp could see vast slides descending in waves from 1,370 metres (4,500 feet) up. The slides turned west at about 610 metres (2,000 feet), headed straight for the inlet instead of proceeding northwest in an old slide chute, and swept

Mt. Rodney, Mt. Superb and Mt. Sir Francis Drake from Len Parker's Bear Bay site on the east side of Bute Inlet, 2011.
Judith Williams photo

old-growth trees into the sea. Chunks of huge fir logs surfaced "loudly and violently from the depths like a broaching pod of whales."

Arne's crew fired up the tug and towed a string of smaller boats to the mouth of the Southgate Slough. Behind them, the waves produced by the slide debris rose to over 50 feet, washing away the camp's saw shop, both porches of the main house and "the fuel dump, containing 500 gallons of gas, thousand-gallon diesel tanks and large eighty-gallon propane tanks." The house itself was untouched.

The Bear River, by Len Parker's old place across the channel, crested at levels not seen for fifty years and rearranged its banks. Late party arrivals found Bute Inlet's entrance plugged with logs and other debris. "A cat could've walked the four miles across the inlet without getting its feet wet!"[72]

Run-of-river powerhouse construction, East Toba River, Toba Inlet.
Phillip Wood photo

Given the inlet's extreme nature, consultation all around is the only strategy that can facilitate entrepreneurial, government, First Nations and environmental actions in Bute, and even then a mountain flank may just decide to roll down on the invaders or shift a river channel. Increasing glacial melt will add new wrinkles to any plan.

Given the inevitability of alteration of the inlet environment by hydro construction, I wondered how an artist might address these issues by making art—but not propaganda. Paintings or photographs of the inlet waterways would always impress, but like glamorous images of brilliantly coloured spawning salmon, they did not seem to inspire serious, ongoing, protective government action. In fact, images of the splendid swimmers seemed to lull the concerned into a sensuous coma. Water in which the salmon spawned and grew would seem to be the primary threatened target of any inlet construction and water export.

I have painted with watercolour paints all my life. What if I collected water from all those systems affected by the hydro and water-bottling licence applications and painted with that alone, not picturing or representing anything, not adding pigment, but allowing the liquids to leave what tone, texture or configuration they could? If I collected again during and after the hydro project, would there be a difference? Could I make an oil painting with just the Bute wax a scientist had suggested was an ideal medium? How big a stretch was it to ask the land itself to reveal a solution to the problem of development?

Bute Inlet water samples, 2010.
Judith Williams photo

On the surface the project seemed more thought experiment than en-actable. I had Bute wax, but getting water samples from such a vast area was a challenge. With the aid of a number of helpers, the water was not only collected, but its collection became a performance of concern, care and focus on a specific terrain. The water paintings I then made created a residue not just of the water (which it did) but, like certain pictographs and petroglyphs, of gentle human intersection with the landscape.

Bute, like the other inlets that thrust their fingers into the mainland and release their essence, is one of the main engines of the coast, sending mineral- and nutrient-laden material down to the hub of islands at the top of the Salish Sea. Since no comprehensive inlet studies have been done, we do not know the full effect that material has on the fertility of this area. Any roads, tunnels, dams or rerouting, and any alteration of water temperature, cannot avoid affecting plant, animal and fish habitat and the water itself. Installing eighteen ROR projects will have considerable impact no matter how well intentioned a construction team may be. The inlet the Homalco, Schnarrs and mountaineers knew will be transformed by hydro towers and lines. Tankers will take water to fill plastic bottles for Detroit or Dubai. Returning tankers will deballast stabilizing water somewhere, and what that water contains only heaven knows—and we, as always, will learn too late.

However, it is important to state that should deals between Plutonic/Alterra/Innergex and the Homalco People be stopped by those who wish to preserve the area, some alternate and equal opportunity must, in conscience, be worked out with the Homalco Band. This contemporary phase of First Nations partnering with commercial interests is to a large degree a result of the provincial government dragging its feet settling territorial claims that have resulted from a failure to finalize treaties in the days of Waddington's road building. In 1863, John Robson, editor of the *British Columbian* and later premier of BC, wrote: "Depend on it, for every acre of land we obtain by improper means, we will have to pay for dearly in the end."

8

LOT A17, RANGE 1, COAST DISTRICT

IT BLEW LIKE HECK UP THERE ALL THE TIME, SUMMER AND WINTER. I DON'T KNOW WHAT HE LIKED THAT AWFUL PLACE FOR, BUT THAT'S WHAT HE CHOSE. THE OLDER HE GOT, THE MORE BUTE BELONGED TO HIM.

—PANSY SCHNARR

Precisely when August added a propeller to his dugout to create the airboat is not clear, but his 1930–1960s periods in Bute were facilitated by the speedy trips up inlet waterways it could provide. Only one very old photo shows the prop installed on a stand in the dugout. It was redrawn to illustrate Maud Emery's 1960 Schnarr article in the Victoria *Colonist*.

August in dugout airboat.
Maud Emery collection

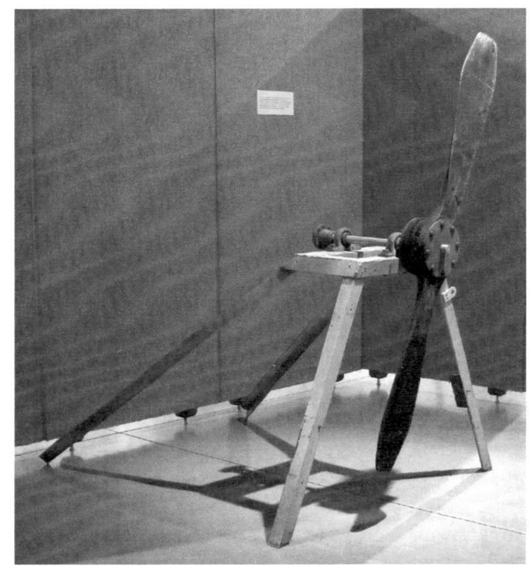

Longboat propeller and stand.
Judith Williams photo

After Pearl died in 2011, Glen Macklin and his father, John, gave me permission to move August's last propeller and its heavy steel stand into our Cortes Island shed to dry slowly and let the wood-bugs inhabiting the ingeniously pieced hardwood hub decamp for the bush; the prop had been rescued in the nick of time.

In the installation *Naming and Claiming: The Creation of Bute Inlet* at the Campbell River Museum in September 2011, the propeller loomed like a long-legged insect confronting August's four-inch steel auger, a facsimile of Charlie's diary, and a pelt of the wolverine August occasionally shot. From the museum collection we added Pansy's Native baskets, a surprising pair of Homalco Band's snowshoes and a plaster Station of the Cross from Church House, loaned to the museum by the band. August's grandsons Norman, Albert and Glen Fair contributed a photo of August taken during their 1970s Bute trip and diagrammed the propeller's position in the last fabricated longboat. They noted previous longboats were hollowed logs.

August and the girls used the propeller-powered canoe to trap up the rivers during the winters they logged at Bear Bay. A 1940 scribbler notes that on March 20 they received $564 from Pappas Furs, and another $517 on April 18. They record a total income of $1,433.42 for two log booms towed south to W.C. and V.E. Kiltz on August 26 and October 25. A tax form lists that year's logging and trapping income as $3,399.88.

Pansy's diary and interviews and Marion's letters indicate how the Schnarrs continued to use

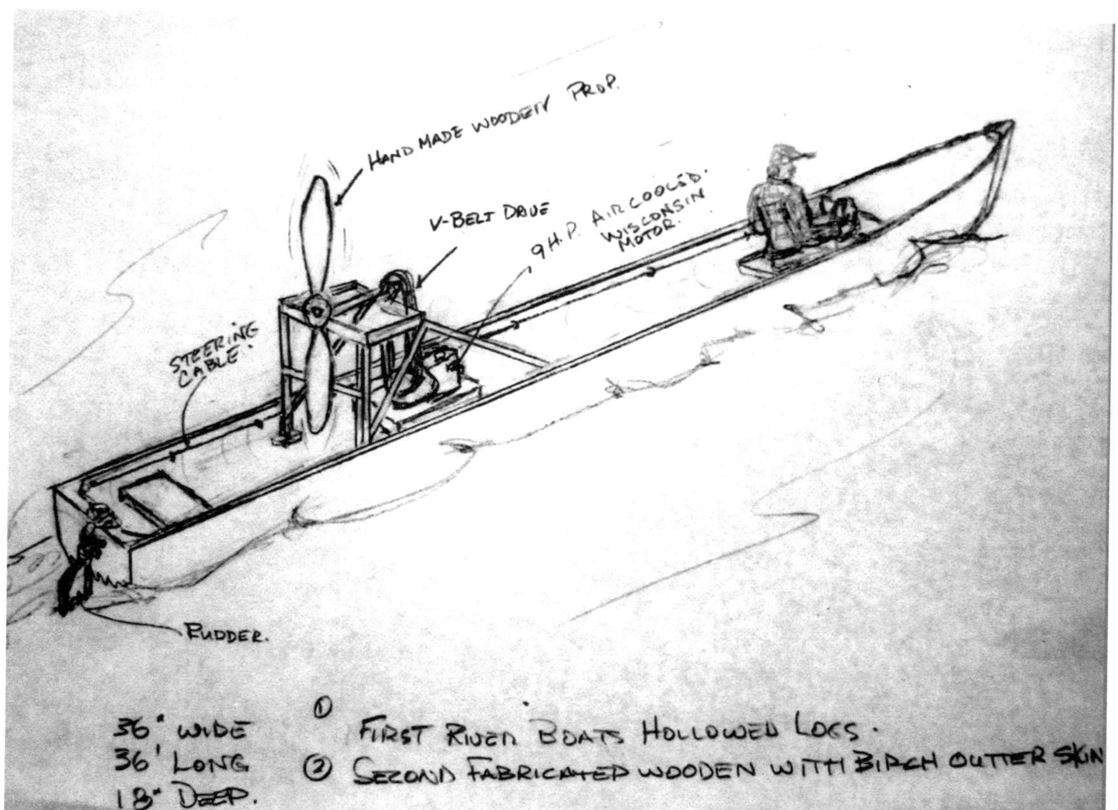

Propeller installation diagram.
Norman, Albert and Glen Fair illustration

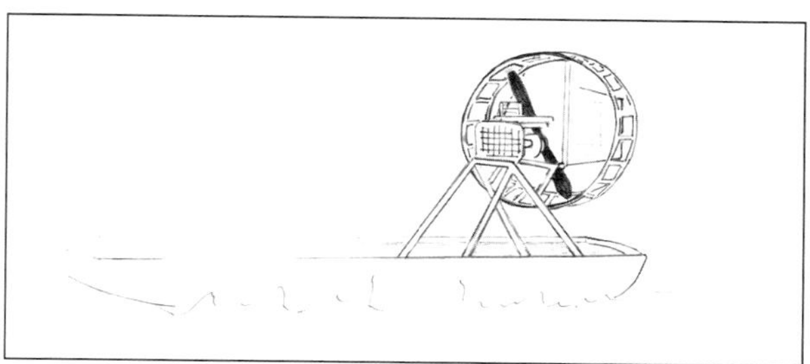

Above: Remembering the longboat moored out in Heriot Bay, David Rousseau sketched the prop's cage and baffles.
Judith Williams illustration from David Rousseau sketch

Left: August and Albert Fair camped in Bute Inlet, c. 1970. Last propeller-driven longboat at right with supplemental "kicker."
Courtesy of Albert Fair

the Landing animal sheds, gardens, fruit trees and berry bushes for themselves and for trade. In 1945 August got a further lease on area EFGH, the Landing's original cultivated area, on which he paid tax and rent. In May 1946 he brought a floathouse up from Fawn Bluff to near the Landing. He'd used it to log another sale after Bear Bay was finished.

In 1947 August heard a lumber outfit was to log in behind the Landing, and in June 1947, when he went there to pick raspberries, he accidently met Mr. Vaux, a log surveyor for the

Glaspie Lumber Company. Papers in the Schnarr fonds relating to an ensuing lawsuit provide a *rough* outline of what happened next.

> I had trouble with [a] logging camp that took my place. I got the best bay in Bute Inlet. I sold one right-a-way [right-of-way]. I'd moved my house 2 miles down inlet out of sight and they moved their buildings in. I saw what they were doing. A year later—there were fruit trees—and I told them not to damage them . . . I saw they had a barge and they were going to move it right thru that area. I went home and got my gun, came back, left it on the beach, went up and got in front of the scow and said "you leave it there!" I went down and got the gun, put it down; they quit. The next day the RCMP came and I explained I never pointed a gun, but the Super, who hadn't even been there, said I had. I explained I had not and made him admit [it], I wasn't going to stand for it! Next year they had to buy [the right-of-way] for $10,000. I never did get it all.[73]

Glen and Albert Fair say August and Len Parker had searched the inlet for minerals as well as for a source of Bute wax and staked a number of claims close to the water. Any operator with a log sale licence located behind their claims had to pay an access fee to cross their land to the timber, as Glaspie was forced to do. August used the money he made this way to buy property in the Rendezvous Islands previously owned by Francis Millard, who ran the Redonda Bay Cannery. When Millard died, his widow wanted to sell, and Len thought he had a deal to receive 10 per cent if he found a buyer. That August would not pay Len this fee was one source of enmity between them.

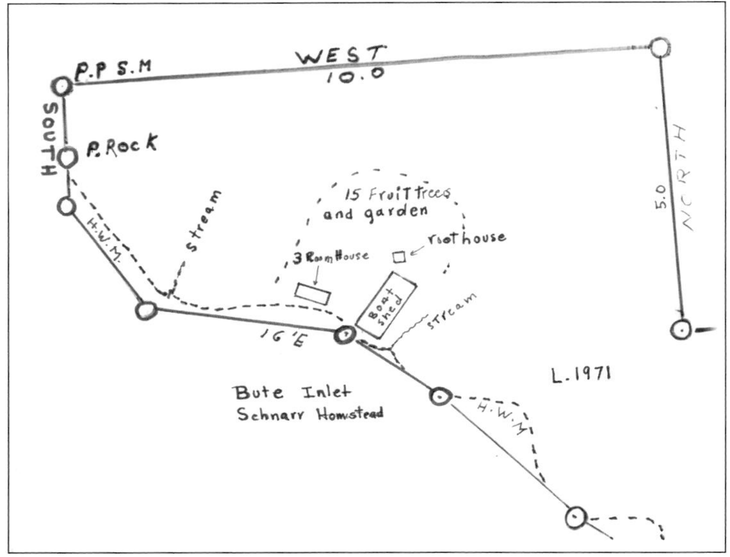

Schnarr's Landing property showing location of house, big boatshed and west orchard. *Judith Williams illustration*

The lengthy lawsuit about the 1947 Landing usage by the Glaspie Lumber Company indicates the single incursion August first allowed the company had excluded the house site, orchard and any cultivated area. The loggers ignored his specifications, tore down his old boatshed, drove through the site with heavy equipment, wrecked the garden and destroyed the orchard. They erected nine buildings above the house site, made the point next to the house into a log dump, and compromised his moorage by starting to drive in the pilings to create a booming ground for logs. August hired a Vancouver lawyer and, in a series of affidavits, claimed they had destroyed forty-two to fifty fruit trees, most of the red and black currant, gooseberry, loganberry, raspberry and blackberry bushes, a 100-square-foot garden and his dead wife's flower garden. The soil built up over twenty years had been moved, and the remainder contaminated by oil.

The case went to the BC Supreme Court in 1948. Len Parker gave evidence that the small bay west of the Landing, where the logging company wanted August to have his house and booms, had bad moorage due to the wind direction. He swore he knew the Landing itself had excellent moorage because he was a long-time resident of the inlet. Letters to August make it clear his lawyer felt he had a strong case, but the legal wrangle continued to be thwarted by Glaspie denials. August claimed $5,000 in damages to his trees, but an "expert" hired by Glaspie said they were worth $500. August had, of course, compromised the case by confronting the loggers and implying he was willing to use his rifle to evict them, and he was served notice not to trespass on his land.

August was certainly hotheaded and known for sticking up logging companies so they would pay for access to their sale, but the logging company significantly overstepped the bounds of the initial agreement and destroyed property he'd hand-built over the years. None of the legal documents evince any understanding of the upcoast economy and how food, tools and services could be valued, loaned and traded. Much commerce was "in kind" one way or another.

There was an implication August lost his rights by not always living in situ. In the days of slow boats, handlogging required the logger to live in proximity to his sale. As Pearl said, the Schnarr buildings were moved all over, and other upcoasters shifted periodically, even seasonally, from one fishing, logging and trapping location to another. August moved houses temporarily from Owen Bay to Bear Bay in 1938 but kept up the Owen Bay potato garden and cabin. He also tended the Landing garden and pruned the trees. The Fawn Bluff floathouse was likely the house moved to the Landing's small outer bay in 1947. That poor moorage was life threatening once the big boat shed, used for hauling and securing the boat in winter, was destroyed by the loggers.

Glaspie Logging prevailed, and its site was later taken over by Taylor Brothers and then Don Hayes Logging. Pansy came with her husband, Lloyd Fair, and son Glen in 1951 to pull out some usable cable from the small northwest bay. In the early 1960s, Lloyd Fair moved into Schnarr's Bay, at Big Creek, east of the Landing, to log. Glen Fair and his wife, Helen, bought a house from the Parrish family for $1,200 and moved it next to Big Creek, and Glen logged there with his dad from 1962 to 1965. After one heavy snow a temperature inversion caused heavy rain, and great boulders crashed down the creek bed by the house. "We stayed awake," Glen said, "ready to leave at any moment." Helen's washhouse on a wooden bridge over the creek was swept away. Dennis Walker's grandson, Vern Logan, towed Lloyd Fair's float camp out of Von Donop Inlet in the late 1960s to a tie-up around Beazley Passage at Surge Narrows. It later caught fire, and Lloyd lost his camp. He was killed in a falling accident, and Pansy married family friend Keith Eddington in 1967.

Pearl said she left home at fifteen, soon after they returned to Bute, and went to Vancouver, then Winnipeg. The Fair brothers say she married "Uncle" Albert Linkletter, part Prairie First Nations, who they thought very well of. "I did good, didn't I?" Pearl used to say. Her copy of Len Parker's *Shadows Lay North*, inscribed "to Pearl and Albert," was a wedding present. After the war the couple had an A-frame logging show north of the Paradise River in Bute. While moving logs one day, Linkletter's boat engine kicked back and flipped him overboard. Unable to swim, he drowned in front of their son, Ronny. Following the accident, an unmoored Pearl seems to have lost contact with August. In the fonds is a letter on two sheets of powder-blue stationery, dated October 12, 1952, from Pasadena, California, where she had cousins. Pearl rather formally addressed her father care of Len Parker:

> Mr. Schnarr: You will no doubt be surprised that I'm writing you thru Mr. Parker. Says you don't like to write, but you can write me can't you please? Have been writing Len but the rascal up and married, guess Mrs. can't let him now. I miss hearing from him but hope he is happy. I am very lonely & unhappy about men, married one, and he proved impossible, wanted me to

support him . . . I have my son to take care of, he gets a little money off his Dady who died, but not enough. I am working & am not too good to work.

Well so much for now, hope I hear from you very soon.

Respect, Pearl. — send me photo here.

August must have written back. Within the next year thirty-year-old Pearl sent a Christmas card to "dear Daddy" from the Lower Mainland.

Dear August. How is everything going with you? I sure hope you are catching a lot of marten. How is Moses? Still alive I hope. I am just fine but I get kinda lonesome for the old place at times. Have been out to Fair's three or four times, he is building two houses to sell. Houses sure are expensive down here. I sure hope to see you down soon. Well so long. Lots of love Pearl.

The same year August received a series of affectionate letters and cards from a Therese Hochmuth. She had stayed with him up Bute, wonders about her potted plants and sends greetings to Mr. and Mrs. Parker. Therese said she left only because of "sprains" to her feet, now cured. They are strange letters full of longing for her "dear friend," love of the wilderness, regret and considerable apprehension.

Albert Fair says August married for a second time, and the new wife demanded he move out of Bute. During the shift some of her dishes were broken, they had a yelling match, August hit her and she sued for divorce.

After Albert Linkletter's death and the 1952 letter, August moved the house Albert and Pearl had been building down from Bute to Heriot Bay for Pearl. Young Albert Fair, Pansy's son, often stayed there with his Aunt Pearl. August moved his own house there too, and jacked it up above high tide west of the Heriot Bay Hotel. Pearl, married to John Macklin, moved a house from Sawmill Bay on Read Island to its present location on Macklin Road.

In the 1970s tapes August said, "I had three daughters, all married now. I'm proud of my family, not one went wrong, that's pretty good for these days. One lived up the hill, another in Campbell River. The one in Victoria married Bert Parker. He's the District Superintendent for BC Hydro. Norman Fair was maintenance man at the pulp mill."

August may have been proud, but some say the girls were a little afraid of him, and Albert Fair characterizes him as so suspicious of people wanting something from him that he never had a close friend. After August died, when Albert and his wife were about to have a child, he told his mother, Pansy, "I don't mind what it is as long as it's not like POP."

"You don't have to worry about that, honey," she said.

It was only then that the boys learned August was not Pansy's father.

Pearl and Marion remained close, but the Fair brothers feel Pansy was sometimes excluded from that relationship. She had, as she said, "become Mother" at twelve.

"This house?" August replied to a question about his Heriot Bay cabin. "I've been here in and out. I was up there, moved down here for school. We were at Owen Bay and moved down here and ended here. There was half a shed, Grace Haines owned it. I bought it for $500, built this up Bute and moved it down. Been here since 60s, sixteen years, but in Bute til 60s. Oh yes!"

When he lived on Quadra, August would bring the longboat in from its mooring at Heriot Bay, load it with supplies and travel up the inlet to continue to trap and explore.

Pansy's sons have owned the Landing since 1971.

9

THE WILD IN US

Mouth of the Southgate River, 2014.
Judith Williams photo

The Schnarr dossier I had built, Charlie Rasmussen's file and the hydro survey, when combined with my photo layouts, created a flowchart of a small group of people moving through place through time. Bute became a storied landscape, each inlet reach revealing the Butites intersecting with waterway geography, its Indigenous peoples, their neighbours and the animal, plant and sea life.

A 1941 school scribbler recorded the Schnarrs' "Miscellaneous expenses" after they'd returned to the inlet. On August 2, 90 gallons of oil, and on the 24th, 123 gallons of gas were purchased at the relatively nearby store in the Homalco village of Church House for a total of $53.00. Now that Pansy's diary had clarified for me how that money was earned, I wanted to take a fresh look at where August and the girls lived and what they encountered moving through the inlet and riverine territory to work. Like Charlie and Pansy, I kept a diary and I photographed what I saw.

August 12, 2014, 9:30. My husband, Bobo Fraser, and I headed our aluminum speedboat, *Tetacus*, north from Cortes Island up Lewis Channel to stay again at Homathko Camp on the river August's skills made his own. At the top of Cortes, Toba Inlet's five rivers send water through Pryce Channel into the Calm/Sutil Channel hub at the Rendezvous Islands to meet the northern flood tide, and a boater enters a grander, more demanding water world of rapids, currents and winds. An unusual number of whales were seen south from here to the gulf that year, transient Biggs orcas chasing seals, and humpbacks sieving up enough sea creatures to keep them around.

Our first stop was Church House, the mainland Homalco village site Lhilhukwem, ("basin shaped"), which became Aupe (U7p) IR #6 and 6A when reserves were fixed. During the Schnarrs' Bute years, a steamer landed passengers and store goods here as well as stopping at the public wharf at the south end of Stuart Island, the older Homalco site Chichxwiyakalh ("clear passage between"). Church House was the main Homalco site by 1900, the last village occupied in their territory until their hatchery and bear-watching lodge were built in Orford Bay.

On the north flank of the bay, a sleek black bear swung its nose, sniffing our scent. At the south end a small path of water filtered through the old village and burial ground to trickle across a beach dotted with cold cream jars, pottery shards, bullet casings and a remarkable number of shoe soles, lined up seaward by the tide like footprints of a fleeing horde.

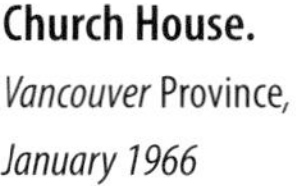

Church House.
Vancouver Province, *January 1966*

Church House church, c. 1992.
Judith Williams photo

One day in the mid-1970s my scheduled floatplane flight from Campbell River to Refuge Cove had stopped here. Four women deplaned with their shopping bags onto a dock and climbed up a ramp to a long pier leading to houses, children and mates in a village where Jesus extended his arms from the church belfry. There had been power lines and roads.

The 1896 church had now collapsed, its moss-covered roof blending into the forest floor. There was nothing to indicate the pier had ever existed. A washing machine eyed us from the porch of a lone standing house, and the small 1960s-era white clinic I'd photographed fronting the church when Tom Soames had run a salmon farm there in the early 1990s was now backed by a dark hole in the bush.

The church marks the Homalco move from Muushkin on Maurelle Island after a "Bute" blew the village down. Non-Indigenous schoolteacher William Thompson and his wife, Emma, built a store and a post office here, and in 1911 tried to pre-empt a fair chunk of Aupe that included the graveyard and several Homalco homes. In 1915 Chief George Harry asked the Royal Commission examining reserve lands to stop this pre-emption, enlarge the Aupe reserve and add offshore Bartlett Island for clams and a sheep range. He requested 10 acres at Bear Bay, a traditional herring fishing station, which was not allowed. The band was allotted 29.7 acres at Aupe, later reduced to 20.08, and the schoolteacher was allowed a small portion. Chief Harry told the commission his people spent the winter at Aupe to meet the priest, but went to X̱we'malhkwu (between Cumsack Creek and the mouth of the Homalco) in the summer and to Pi7pḵnech (Orford Bay) for chum salmon in August and September.[74]

The Thompson family continued to run the store and sell the gas the Schnarrs bought. Many Church House residents went to work in the logging industry and at Redonda Bay Cannery, which closed in the late 1940s. The current Homalco chief, Darren Blaney, says Church House suffered a final financial blow in the late 1960s when the federal government imple-

Above left: Homalco men Albert Georgeson and Johnny Blaney carving a racing canoe at Church House.
Courtesy of Homalco First Nation

Above right: Church House 2006.
Cathy Campbell photo

Below: The hand of Jesus in the grass at Church House, 1990s.
Judith Williams photo

mented the Davis Plan, an attempt to downsize the fishing industry through licence restrictions, which penalized small, family-operated boats with general fishing licences. Unable to meet the requirements, twenty-four of twenty-six Homalco boats lost their licences, and families lost their livelihood. Although some residents stayed into the 1970s, and there were attempts to preserve the church in the '90s, the Homalco Band now occupies a site at 1218 Bute Crescent, south of Campbell River. Each time we came to Church House there were fewer people and fewer buildings. Jesus fell from his belfry, and his broken hands lay in tall grass. Like the village, the inlet emptied out as small-scale economic activities practised by the truly independent disappeared.

North, at Fawn Bluff, where the inlet narrows, a kind of magic begins. The silt-charged water becomes a luminous jade path, and seven-, eight-, nine-thousand-foot mountains unfold great scoured-out creek beds and lift glaciers into the sky. A marine sample taken where August anchored in the '20s and logged in the '40s was a vibrant cocktail of fresh water from the Coast Range glaciers mixed with seawater flooding from the north through the Arran Rapids across channel.

Water collection, Rainbow Creek Falls, 2011.
Cathy Campbell photo

Fresh water makes up 2.5 to 2.75 per cent of all the water in the world, and 1.75 to 2 per cent of it is stored for our convenience in glaciers, ice and permanent snowfields. There was almost no snowpack in 2014 compared with what Bobo and I had seen in our 2010 and 2011 Bute expeditions, and now exposed ridges of glacial ice gleamed pale ultramarine in midday light. On August 23, 2011, one of our companions, Cathy Campbell, got soaked at Raindrop Creek Falls when we tried to get close enough to collect water. Wind generated by the long, powerful falls blew the boat away. Now the thinnest veil of water trickled onto the surface.

North of Boyd Point an incoming helicopter swung a dangling lanyard over our heads. Moored at shore was the float-camp barge I'd watched being rebuilt at the Whaletown dock the previous winter. Logging had begun again next to Schnarr's Landing, and a new bridge had been constructed over Big Creek where water ran down off the south flank of 2,673-metre (8,770-foot) Mt. Sir Francis Drake.

August had climbed up Big Creek Valley to make a rough, swivelling panoramic photo series above the inlet. Looking at these glacier photos in 1977, he said, "I'm up on Needles Peaks, looking down, 7,000 feet above where I lived. Hot day!"

West of Big Creek, on the long, south-facing gravel beach Pearl said was unique to the inlet, flattish pink and grey stones mounded up to silvered beach logs. This was Schnarr's Landing homestead. It's said salmon roll against these smooth rocks to remove lice before going to spawn in Big Creek, and trout follow along to snitch their eggs. But because the surrounding land

Collaged photos from Needles Peaks.
August Schnarr photos. Images MCR 20447-68, 20447-70, 20447-71 courtesy of the Museum at Campbell River

rise is so abrupt, eggs in low spawning beds are vulnerable to smothering by silt runoff from avalanche-prone slopes being logged again.

The sea was calm and the beach approach easy enough, but thickly suspended silt roiled and clouded the water as if the world was still forming, melting or mixing into something new, which, of course, it was; Bute always exhibiting the world in process. Above the gravel shore, behind a dark hole in the beach brush, rough boulder stairs led up to an alder-shadowed A-frame that Pansy's sons maintain. The building sat on a flat silty bench below a sunny cleared area. Plastic over screen windows hung in tatters, but the floor seemed sound, and I thought the building would not collapse if the tarp under the mossy shakes stayed intact.

In August's old photos of the first house, which sank, two sheds sit right at the beach with two houses hauled up behind. A garden appears to run up to an orchard at the height of the present A-frame. A new survey map (Lot 1971) records a three-room house and a huge boatshed for

Schnarr's Landing animal shed with young Pearl and Marion. The log boom points south, down inlet, c. 1930.
August Schnarr photo. Image MCR 6699 courtesy of the Museum at Campbell River

hauling out the gasboat during winter in front of a root house, garden and fifteen-tree orchard. Glaspie did such extensive bulldozing that the landscape was transformed. No fruit trees were now visible. The Fairs demolished Glaspie's remaining building to build the A-frame. A wavy-grilled '50s truck missing its engine and a blue door refusing to fall into its collapsed building are secondary stage remains giving little sense of Pansy's "old place" gardens where she picked apples for jelly in 1938 and '39.

The Schnarrs' first house was east of a small point where Glaspie established his log dump. The only remaining sign of occupation on the beach was a rotting piling at the east end of the property, a tied-in log below the dump and a solitary, sea-worn shard of green glass. Even the new logging show was temporary. I'll find that floating bunkhouse, helicopter and landing barge again someday at a new log sale when I investigate an out-of-the-way arm or inlet.

We continued up the inlet, motoring past Purcell Point and west into Bear Bay. The light mist had burned off and the mountain peaks sharpened against the sky. A floathouse was jacked up on pilings below Mt. Smith. Could this be where the Schnarrs moved ashore in 1938?

During our 2011 expedition we had tied up to a buoy at Bute Inlet Lodge, south of Bear River. Owners Brian and Mark Gage ran Len Parker's place as a wilderness exploration business. Here Len Parker logged or wrote in the front cabin while Laurette painted in the back shack during the 1970s. There is now a small Homalco reserve on the river's north side.

Below left: Vintage truck grille.
Judith Williams photo

Below right: The Landing A-frame.
Judith Williams photo

In the winter of 2015, a few months after our journey, Bute continued its rearrangement of the landscape. A hydraulic eruption caused by new logging blew out the soil below the A-frame, opening a trench under the floor studs on the left side of the building. The soil shelf Glaspie bulldozed out from the Schnarr orchard and garden collapsed and water and soil, running out from under the front porch, flushed the path I'd climbed up down to the beach. A small area of First Nations shell midden was exposed where Glen Macklin had earlier found what he termed "big stone daggers."

View under the washed-out A-frame, 2015.
Jeanette Taylor photo

Len Parker's two houses, Bear Bay, 2011.
Judith Williams photo

Arcing *Tac* north from Bear Bay toward the Homathko River made the Bute Mountain massif seem to slide left and half block the two-winged Bute Glacier. The visible left wing, hanging above the river mouth like a shaggy pelt, no longer completely blanketed the bald rock as it had done in mountaineer Tom Fyles's 1930 *Alpine Journal* photo. Earlier, in the 1920s, August took a photo from the river that showed the glacier with snowpack. He was afloat close to the present location of Homathko Camp dock, on an initial section of Waddington's road. Each time I came up the river the glacier had retreated more.

Above: Stuffed sea lion head on the wall in Len Parker's cabin, 2011.
Judith Williams photo

Left: View of Bute Glacier from the Homathko River, c. 1920s.
August Schnarr photo. Image MCR 14395 courtesy of the Museum at Campbell River

Above: Bobo Fraser piloting *Tac* at the Homathko entrance; Bute Glacier ahead, 2014.
Judith Williams photo

Left: Bute Mountain from Mt. Rodney, 1930.
Photo by Tom Fyles

Above: Dean Potter jumped off Bute Mountain in a wingsuit for a 2011 *National Geographic* documentary to publicize the grandeur of the area for its protection.[75] Photo looks toward the Whitemantle Range.
Mikey Shaefer photo

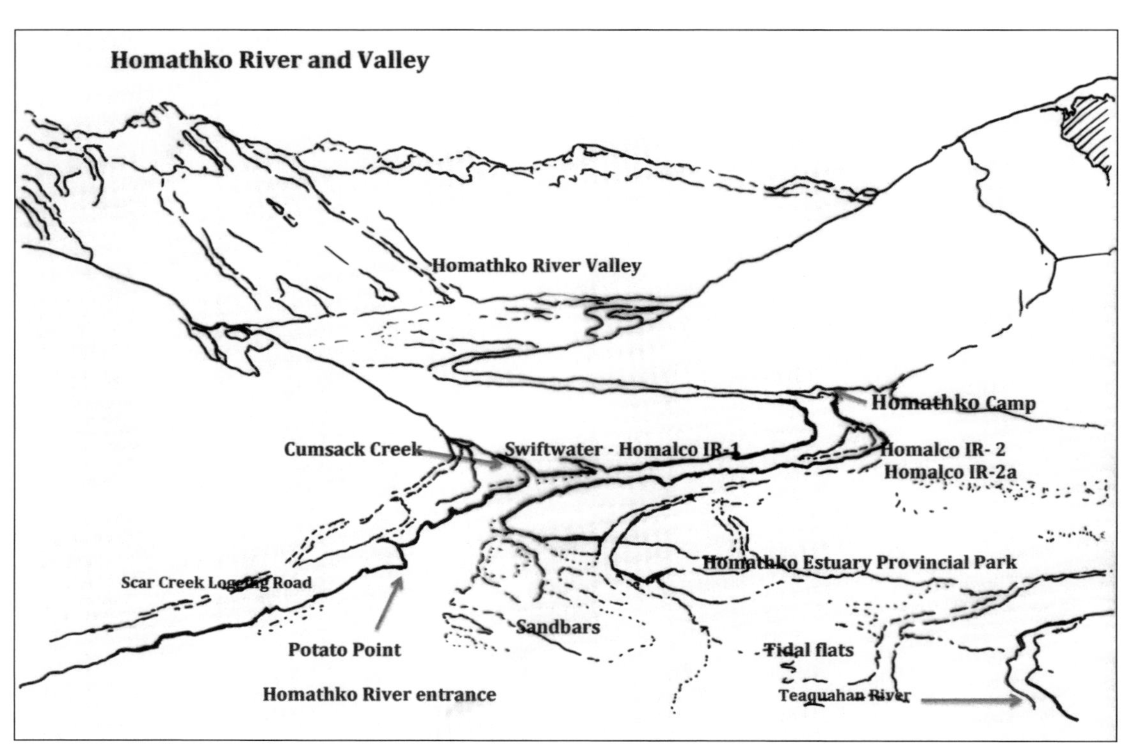

Right: Homathko Valley.
Judith Williams illustration

At the south side of the Homathko River mouth, a line of pilings for tying in log booms marks Scar Creek Logging's sort and dump. Now truck logging is closed on this side of the Homathko, the booms have been pulled away and our usual route along that shore into the river proved hazardous. A rock fall below the logging road had cut into the flow and built up a higher river bar. For the first time we ran aground. An oar stuck into creamy, opaque water indicated the depth was a meagre foot. The river swirled a whole leafy cottonwood out into the inlet through what had to be a deeper channel on the north side. I pried us off in that direction, and we drifted back out into Waddington Harbour past a long, new sandbar.

The rising tide allowed us to motor into the river past a 20-foot log stuck into the mucky north shore like a javelin. At the entrance to Cumsack Creek another bar had built up out into the river from the old village site of Swift Water, and at the first valley switchback the water ran fiercely at Homathko Camp dock. The river toggles down Homathko Valley through seasonally shifting sandbars studded with interlocked debris. Passage with an outboard is chancy even in our shallow-draft aluminum boat.

Tac was forced against this flow and in behind the small dock Chuck Burchill had secured in a back eddy. I grabbed the rope hanging from a dock ring, wrapped and tied, snugged in the stern and climbed onto the quivering finger float with the bowline. The river leapt enthusiastically up through a steel mesh surface welded over the four 16-inch steel pipes that constitute the main dock it was attached to, and I gained the ramp with relief. The dock is clever enough and well secured onshore, but the river flows so ceaselessly, implacably and with such indifferent force that I view it with total and humble respect. I am not going to do well if I fall in.

4:30: Safe in camp. Chuck trucked us up to the trailer we had in 2010. Five beds, bathroom, shower and a kitchen we never use. Sheron Burchill's son Wayne cooked pork chops and prepared a big salad from the garden lush with corn, beets, tomatoes, cukes and blackberries. We ate on the lawn in front of the cookhouse. Only a glassed porch has been added since our 1991 visit.

I showed them the one picture I'd found of August in the airboat. Chuck explained how the Homathko monitoring systems indicate it has the third-largest volume of flow of BC rivers, and we considered how laborious and dangerous it would have been to pole upriver alone before August invented the propeller mechanism.

Chuck recognized the location of August's photograph of Charlie Rasmussen at Giant Rock from his hikes. Unless they fly, people intending to go up the left side of the valley past Homathko Canyon must still hike past the massive slab.

We slept in the back bedroom of the trailer, within earshot of the huge sound of Camp Creek, harnessed by Chuck to supply any amount of hydropower to the camp.

August 13. Mist on the river brought me out to the dock at six, where drifting fog slunk down the sides of the Homathko. Its force, still in freshet, underlines August's singular river skills in all seasons. The melt from the Coast Range and the 30-mile-diameter Homathko Icefield begins

Homathko Camp dock, 2014.
Judith Williams photo

in July, but Chuck showed us a photo of Wayne standing on four feet of ice in the much lower winter river, right in front of the dock.

In 1929, August and Charlie came upriver in October and left the boat blocked up out of the water at the south end of the canyon. When Charlie returned on December 8, he found the chocks holding the longboat had shifted in the river rise caused by rain. Descending the Homathko ten days later in the boat, after the higher freeze-up, he notes that he encountered ice jams. Robert Homfray wrote of finding salmon encased in ice balls along the riverbanks around November 15 in 1861. Even today it can be so bitterly cold up the valley that the combination of days of hoarfrost and 160-kilometre-an-hour (100-mile-an-hour) winds dehydrates trees to the point that the slightest spark can create a fire in the dead of winter. Perhaps the trees Charlie described setting on fire were dry as tinder.

Negotiating the river at any time was a challenge, but silt now rebuilding the mouth would not have been such an issue prior to logging and the increasing glacial melt. When August came to trap in low-water season, usable channels may have been more obvious. Still, his and Marion's ability to safely navigate that canoe was and is still impressive.

The previous day's intense flow had made me apprehensive, but the sunlit mist now moving upriver, lifting and blurring the far edge of trees, was enchanting. It would be a fine day. Chuck quickly laid out a logging camp breakfast: grapefruit, eggs, bacon, sausage, toast and their homemade raspberry jam. He was eager to get underway so I could photograph an unrecorded pictograph.

My coastal journeys have led to a fascination with First Nations painted pictographs and carved petroglyphs, signs still in situ of the mind at work in wilderness, the antithesis of decontextualized museum artifacts. Any culture's engagement with landscape becomes layered with various cognitive maps relating to space, time and event. Indigenous people marked their territory with carved or painted images meaningful to them and their neighbours. In 1792 Thomas Heddington drew *The Village of the Friendly Indians*, which William Alexander rendered into watercolour and then engraved to be printed in Vancouver's journals (see image on page 104). August recorded what he cared about in his territory in a medium of his time. Visiting rock art in situ, or a reproduction's or a photo's location, tells how people relate to that world using their iconography and the materials at hand. Interestingly, rock art does not allow one to stay fixed on image alone, since the rock surface also holds our interest, and we flip back and forth between image and ground, more aware of context than we usually are viewing a photograph or engraving. For most Indigenous groups the rock itself was alive and informed any painted or carved image, which was as much a residue of a dream, performance or event as it was a picture in the sense that we might think of them.

Stonefall, pictograph site, Homathko Valley, 2014.
Judith Williams photo

Alder is quickly filling in the Homathko Valley roads, but we could drive to the landing strip Chuck kept groomed just above camp. They'd had fifteen planes of a flying club here overnight on August 8. At the south end of the strip a startling stone outcrop rippled a series of galleries up out from a forest mass. The elegantly rounded granitic overhangs, 36 to 46 metres (120 to 150 feet) above the valley floor, are a glacial and epiglacial landform shaped by the passage of glaciers and partially polished by meltwater.

In 1991, when Sam Smythe drove us up the valley on extensive logging roads then in full use, I had seen red marks at one gallery level and taken two fast photos. Chuck once climbed up beside this outcrop with his daughter and rappelled down to the paintings, but the footing was too steep for photography. I could now see two panels with red marks, but a small pine in front of the bottom of the larger panel obscured the main red form. No recognizable image was decipherable, even with a telephoto lens. Alder had grown tall along the road where I took the 1991 shots, and I could now see the rock formation only from the landing strip or faintly as we came upriver to the camp dock. Chuck said it could be seen from other places in the valley. The determined painter(s) must have hung from above with carefully prepared ochre and brush in hand.[76]

Painted stone pictograph galleries, Homathko Valley, 2014.
Chuck Burchill photo

"I can put you on Potato Point," Chuck had said the previous night. We'd been talking about Jack Mould's dynamiting of the protected burial site at IR #3V and his disappearance in 2007. Jack, inclined to dynamite at the whiff of a gold tell, had set off a massive blast that reverberated up the valley to camp, and Chuck boated down to discover the sound's source. Seeing the desecration, he called the RCMP. Jack said he'd been looking for "artifacts" for two "Doctors" who were nowhere to be found. When he disappeared, the RCMP arrived at camp to assure themselves nobody from there was responsible.

After the picto shoot we motored downstream in the camp's aluminum herring skiff. Chuck cruised past Potato Point to indicate the sighting from the Southgate to the point that could guide a boat through the correct river channel. Landmarks are essential; the totally opaque water makes it impossible to see sandbars or deadheads. Then he turned upstream and bunted the skiff against Potato Point's slimy rocks. Wayne pulled me up off the boat bow onto this mound August had passed each time he went upriver. Between tree stands was a razed area where Jack had landed a skidder from a barge and cleared a way uphill. Regrown, the chest-high salmonberry and coastal black gooseberry were so dense we climbed up the side between trees and fallen logs.

At the top of the rise I stopped, smelled . . . *dead*! Whose bones had we trodden on? There were large old trees on the mound that could have held burial boxes—now fallen—if that was what the Homalco used. Where the mound levelled back toward a cliff that might have provided niches for bones, Mould had blasted a rectangular hole, now half filled with water. The back and one side of the cavity suggested a different matrix had been inset within a darker stone, and Jack, suspecting the presence of gold, had blown it out. It was nasty and illegal, but the Homalco chief at the time did nothing. Mind you, some of Jack's gold patrons were reported to be a very rough crew. Anything Jack may have found remains as mysterious as his disappearance up the Southgate.

The vista from the mound across the estuary to the stark, sheer face of Mount Bute was dramatic, and a burial position away from flood-prone village houses built on pilings must have been comforting. There was a swath of what looked to be a slender version of edible arrowgrass growing below in a back eddy.

In the late 1970s, Homalco elders Ambrose Wilson and Tommy Paul told researchers Randy Bouchard and Dorothy Kennedy that Potato Point was known as mimekw'maakw'a, literally meaning "a bunch of little corpses" (because it was the burial ground for the X̱we'malhkwu village), or ch'ilhep, meaning "tangled brush or wood" (because the area had grown over with tangled brush difficult to get through). Paul, born around 1900, said that "in his grandfather's time the Homalco caught seals off Potato Point using special large-mesh cedar-bark nets similar to modern gill-nets."[77] The contemporary name is a bit of a conundrum. Although river meets inlet here, Waddington Harbour has a deep layer of fresh water, and native wapato, a broader-leafed arrowgrass that produces a tuber known as Indian potato, might have grown here, providing the name. But Southgate settlers introduced potatoes to the valley by at least the 1890s, and Indigenous people had learned even earlier to grow them to sell to ships.

Chuck boomed the skiff upstream to the end of Cumsack Creek. A pale blue heron extended up from a stand of silt-coated skunk cabbage and floated across the stream in a stunningly fluid motion no still camera could capture. Later, at the stone table Chuck installed next to the camp greenhouse, I tried to find some painted equivalent for that elemental vision as the opaque river flowed and flowed, unstoppable and irretrievable as the heron's flight.

At dinner Chuck asked if the Homalco made and traded eulachon oil. A visiting Fisheries officer had stated that this habitat was inappropriate, and although there were some eulachon, they did not contain much oil. Interestingly, a 1994–99 Fisheries and Oceans stock assessment study cited Bute Inlet as one of sixteen main eulachon-spawning areas of the coast.[78] If there were eulachon but little grease, what was traded to the Interior along the trails Knewstubb noted?

We discussed other Bute mysteries, like a fish wheel installed on the Homathko that indicated sockeye, contrary to other data, spawned at the head of the inlet due to its deep layer of fresh water. Saltwater steelhead, Chuck said, do not spawn in the Teaquahan as is generally thought, but go there to hunt—perhaps the exiting baby eulachon, whose parents only spawn in its Galleon Creek tributary. Chuck added that fishing guide Randy Killoran shows him trout he catches in high lakes where Charlie and August caught them in 1929. Chuck longed to get up past the canyon to see the newly reported remnants of the underground houses where Homfray and his crew were sheltered by the Tŝilhqot'in in 1861.

I stayed late alone at the table in front of the cookhouse. Cloud moved like a hunting creature in and around and over ridges, pushing apart mountain ranges that read as a mass during the day. Years earlier I'd sat here in hot sun as the glacier across the river dripped down to become a waterfall. There was no snow at this camp in the past winter and blue ice glowed at the glacier's fore-edge. I tried to draw but could not capture the popping dimensionality. The group of minimalist paintings I did with the inlet's water came closer to some essential experience for me; not picturing, but laying another process beside nature's grand gestures. However, drawing

Jack Mould's barge, Southgate River.
Courtesy of Judith Williams/Cathy Campbell

helps learn form that can release meaning the landscape encodes. When it was too dark to see I went to bed, waking again when a moon re-illuminated the glacier.

August 14. Shafts of morning light separated peak, ridge and glacier mass. A strand of cloud dropped slowly down a dark mound, met another and together they slipped out of a hung valley, 1.5 kilometres (5,000 feet) above me, and moved upriver.

After breakfast, Bobo and I slid downstream and across the silken harbour to the mouth of the Southgate River. A new road had been blasted down to the edge of the cliff, marking its south entrance. Raw fractured rock spiralled up to become a rough track east that dropped down to a small camp set where we entered the river proper. The cliff is the log dump for Interfor's long road to Icefall Creek Valley, where huge trees, too big for helicopter retrieval, still stand. A forestry engineer had told us privately that the road and camp were built when salmon were spawning. The blatant prominence of the devastation was staggering. But the road building was closed until fall, and we were the only people moving within the upper inlet's splendour.

The flooding tide made the river choppy where it met the sea, but upstream it swirled glassily through a lazy bend where a cabin hid in thick alder. Farther up, at shallow rapids where the

old northside logging road came down to the bank, Jack left his dog and truck and was never seen again. The tracks of a large creature lined along the opposite sandbar.

Bobo drove northward out of the river across what can be a drying flat of mired logs to a massive rock pier running from Jack's old barge. We tied to the remains of a metal dock strung out to a piling. A bag lay open on the dock spilling out the mud being hand-dug from the river for shipment, a pilot had told Chuck, to a cosmetic company. The long pier road was dotted with bear and wolf scat, and huge tracks from newly introduced elk were churned into mud hedged by encroaching alder. A wispy, bug-spun cage contained crisp orange leaves and grubs wiggling with ugly potential. A sign added to Jack's barge promised twenty-four-hour video surveillance, but the back door flapped invitingly open and shut in the breeze. I waved at the unseen camera and faced out to the slough behind the stone pier—the location, Jack claimed, of the sunken Spanish galleon. Dynamically angled ropes and nets framed the focus across glaucous-green water to House Mountain at the Homathko's mouth, air slipping through swooping swallow feathers the only sound.

Above: Animal tracks on the bank of the Southgate River.
Judith Williams photo

Below left: Plastic skull and bones.
Judith Williams photo

Below right: Wooden cross.
Judith Williams photo

Dock and boats, Southgate River mouth.
Judith Williams photo

I wandered out to Jack's arrangement of dog graves, plastic bones and skulls. The silt bank was collapsing there, and I had the sense it would eventually drop the bones into a fibreglass boat, already capsized below, and eventually entomb them deeper within the silt, as Jack said the galleon was preserved, a plastic offering for the ages.

Bobo was sitting on a stack of wooden pallets. "The collection of batteries is still here," he called.

As I turned, around me rose a period installation, a backwoods cousin to a reconstructed room at the Metropolitan Museum in New York: the dining room designed by Robert Adam in 1761 for John Stuart, 3rd Earl of Bute, when he was prime minister of England.[79] The carefully stacked batteries, five eras of trucks stuffed with vintage chair and machine parts, generations of outboard engines, a blue plastic tarp door and the barge tool-wall were all as much elements of the Mould Room as an Adam chair, nude statues and Boussan rug were of the other. I snapped photos of nets, a boat with its motor in a barrel, a tractor, elk prints, wolf scat and another spun bouquet of wiggling grubs stuck like a wrapped flower arrangement in a tree, objects and processes of our time displayed against a background of implacable stony grandeur. I was as alive with inspiration as August designing his propeller, and as mad as Jack dreaming of gold.

East, up the old logging road, the cabin seen from the river was composing down, burdened with moss and alder leaves. Written on the entrance wall was "Slumach/Jackson Mines Ltd.," the name of Mould's company. Underneath were listed the gold-survey periods from 1952 to 1993. The floor of the inner room, containing the painting of dated gravestones below a spiral mountain, with men wildly digging in a graveyard by lamplight—a projection and perhaps map of Jack's gold dream—was collapsing.

Period room image, 2014.
Judith Williams photo

Left: Detail of cabin wall painting, Southgate River, 2011.
Mike Moore photo

Right: Jack Mould's gold survey timeline, 2014.
Judith Williams photo

Across the inlet, in an open cove of Bear Bay, I saw a tidal shuffling of black/brown branches and twigs loosely distributed across a lemon-lime aquatic plain. Bewitched, I slalomed north through the random debris at full speed, making sharp turns like an exuberant skier to avoid the dark wood. As the prop cut through the sea, some refraction of light caused my wild wake to crest as translucent lemon sorbet. It was my fancy that Bute wax, which once in extreme weather rolled around here as 16-inch wax balls, had returned as dessert.

Once before, heading south in a similar afternoon light, something, perhaps those waxy marine lipids, suspended as they must be somewhere, caught that brightness and reflected it back as a curiously citrus surface. Captivated by the tone, I'd scented the Bute wax trail for a moment. Here it was again.

Len Parker's poem asked what August sought within the mountains. I think August found and engaged with wonders like my lemon-lime plain, places of mind where his wildness, like mine, could live.

The tide had fallen. Back at the Homathko's mouth, getting Chuck's Southgate alignment wrong, I grounded us in eight inches of water. Bobo stepped off the stern and with hefty lifts and pushes shifted the boat into deeper water. As he got back in the boat, one of his Crocs stuck in the muck. It popped up and bobbed along after us as the river flushed us back out to the harbour. Giggling a bit hysterically, I boated it with the fishnet. Bobo correctly lined up Potato Point and we motored upriver, alarmingly close to the north shore's beached trees. He docked well despite the day's sensory overload. I went to the trailer and fell into a lemon-lime reverie.

The Cumsack Range, Homathko Valley.
Judith Williams photo

At dinner a lone cowbird followed Bobo up the stairs into the cookhouse and then ate cake sitting on Wayne's plate. It pecked my arm in a confident way and sat on the back of my chair like a long-time pal. Have they learned to hang out with the Southgate elk in lieu of cattle?

Too exhilarated to sleep, I lay in bed letting the creek's rush sort through swallows' nests, motors, netting, Spanish galleons and August's photos of the Moulds with dead things for the period room in my head. If I added August's 1926 photo of Charlie in front of this cabin to the survey dates I found there, I had the Mould room's timeline.

Charlie Mould, 21, with string of marten, 1926.[80]
August Schnarr photo

August 15. Thick fog on the morning river.

The moment Chuck undid our boat lines, the current hurried us down a blurred waterway and out toward great sunlit cloud strands over the Southgate. The silence was enormous. At Bear Bay we slipped deeper into nothing. Bobo kept his eye on the compass, and I eventually sighted the ghost of a shore, certain we should be at Purcell Point, but an impossible left opening appeared.

"South?" I asked.

"Yes," he said, "yes!"

We'd curved left, then right, and had to be at the west shore, outside Mellerish Point.

Pictograph panel, Orford Bay, 2011.
Judith Williams photo

Down inlet, at Orford Bay, the fog evaporated. I remembered Pearl saying she'd seen "hieroglyphics" way up on the bluff next to the river mouth. Stopping to look for what she'd seen, what the Homalco inhabitants of Pi7pk̲nech had seen and painted, we entered a deeper inlet past. Orford Bay is the only Bute Inlet site manifesting a combined ancient and contemporary Homalco presence. On the south side, a dock and road led to their Bears of Bute Lodge. At the river mouth on the north side was a tall cliff. Parallel red ochre lines 7.6 metres (25 feet) above high-tide mark formed themselves into a serpentine something that I very much wanted to call a creature. Behind a limbed fir tree to its left was painted an extended lipstick-red zigzag.

Projecting image recognition from our contemporary world onto traditional Indigenous images can lead one so far astray that the original intent is lost. I knew I needed to curb what I thought I saw in order to experience what the painter intended. However, if these red marks depicted something serpentine, could it be a Homalco variation of Sisiutl, the two-headed serpent found in Kwakwaka'wakw iconography, or a completely different concept? I knew a wooden Coast Salish memorial box from the Musqueam People of the Fraser River is supported by a spiritually powerful, two-headed serpent they call Sillhqey (S?i:lqey).

The gaze of the Kwakwaka'wakw Sisiutl (one of their highest-ranking crests) was said to petrify the observer. Conversely, a piece of its skin could confer riches and power, or its blood could strengthen warriors. Were these red marks that contradictory something with a long-tongued mouth at the right end and a horned head—or was that a flippered tail or legs or flukes?—at the other? Which was the head?

In the 120-year-old dance hall at Gwai Yi in Kingcome Inlet, a Sisiutl is carved as the main beam. It has a face in the middle and long-tongued mouths at each end. The house itself illustrates the story of a Sisiutl in the river instructing a man how to build the first Gukwdzi or Big House. Villagers told me that snaky creature then climbed out and draped itself between the uprights to become the still-existing beam—thereby creating the time- and mind-bending Möbius strip of narrative I have come to accept in First Nations stories.[81]

But what was I actually looking at here? There are four separate images at Orford. On the left is the horizontal red zigzag with one horned head on the right and a flipped tail. The three-

Zigzag "serpent," Orford Bay, 2014. *Judith Williams illustration*

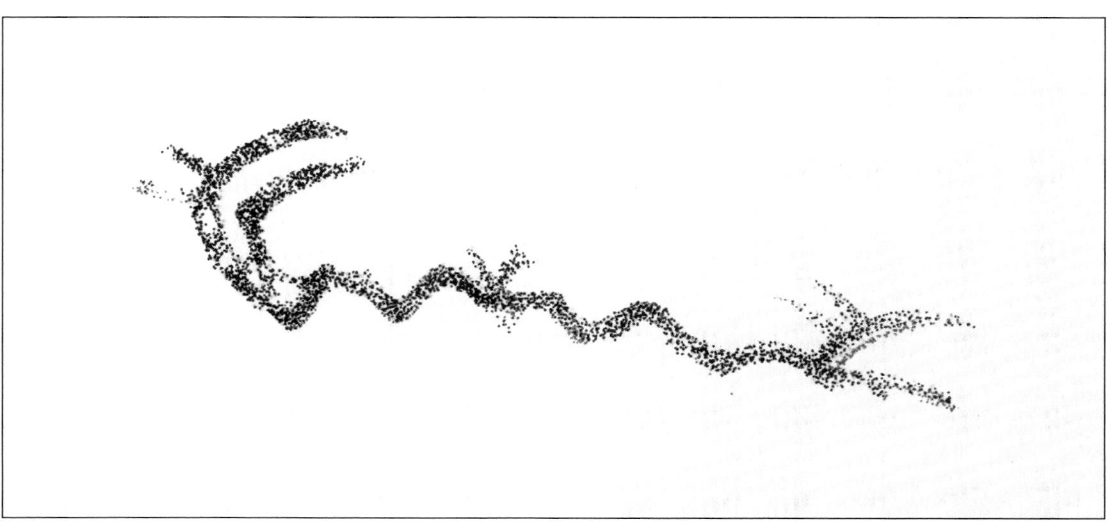

foot-by-six-foot double-outlined serpent to its right could have just one head at the left and a tail where I saw a head and tongue. Was that a "blow hole" in the middle of each serpent's back, suggesting whale-like creatures? The middle of the central Orford image was obscured by a branch, but assuming it was a whole creature, was it something seen, imagined, hallucinated or culturally cultivated? Despite seeming a serpentine representation, was it so symbolic I might never guess its meaning?

Could these images be cousins to a Klahoose pictograph of a serpent ridden by a man, his arms outstretched, gleeful at his daring prowess, in Homfray Channel? During my 1986 visit to the channel that winds around the back of East Redonda to Toba Inlet, Sliammon Chief Roy Francis stood on the ledge with one arm identically outstretched as Klahoose Chief Danny Louie said, "My dad used to tell a story of the sea serpent of Homfray Channel." That painted serpent, floating above a wild-haired figure and men spearing a seal from a canoe, makes use of a stone bulge for a big head with a natural indentation painted red for an eye. This splendid gallery poses more than just the questions about content, date and technique. Why do we make

Homfray Channel pictograph gallery, East Redonda Island, 1986. Helen Hanson (most likely), left; Roy Francis, centre; Danny Louie, right. *Judith Williams photo*

images and what are we doing in that act and to what degree does exposure to drawn, painted or filmed representations affect how we perceive the world? For Danny, the picto verified his father's ancient story that stood as proof of his belonging to this territory.

At Orford, below and to the right of the upper images, almost lost behind a small maple, a humanoid holds what might be a small snaky thing. Could this be the serpent-visioning protagonist, the commissioner of the images or the painter? Was the pictograph made to mark the holder of spiritual power derived from something serpentine? Does being present with the images in itself mean contact with the power of the depicted? I tried to enter the mindset of this image-maker, as I want to enter the mindset of August Schnarr when he reduced Charlie to the most transitory significance against Giant Rock, or whoever captured the shared potent glances of the teenage Marion with the cougar Leo.

Below the Orford zigzag is a shallow cave with a small hearth containing calcinated and

Above: Orford River pictograph of humanoid, adapted from photo and Archaeology Site Report #EdSf-1 1967.
Judith Williams illustration

Right: Cave at Orford River pictograph site.
Cathy Campbell photo

burnt mammal bones, burnt wood, mussel shells, basketry fragments and a small concentration of red ochre, the pigment used to paint most pictographs worldwide, and locally procurable up Galleon Creek. An inscrutable petroglyph is pecked into a boulder directly outside the shelter.

Naturally occurring red ochre (anhydrous iron oxide) was sometimes burned in the form of limonite to intensify its colour. Some say it was mixed with fat or blood or a salmon egg binder. Recently it has been claimed women chewed the eggs to emulsify them before they were mixed with pigment. It's possible to make excellent egg tempera this way. A palette ledge near the Homfray pictograph complex was used for grinding and mixing paint onsite, and although I sent a sample from it to Conservation Canada, no binding agent could be found. Since it is already oxidized, iron oxide does not fade if it is fixed by the natural mineral runoff that inhibits dark lichen growth and keeps the stone surface whitish. However, it can be buried by the mineral runoff, rock shards can spall off or, if unfixed, exposed pigment can run to blushing mush. Access to the Orford ledges is difficult except from above, but there is the slenderest toehold, and the rocks provide sufficient overhang to allow for the mineral runoff to fix pigment. The central pictograph may have been painted by someone supported from above. Experts have been at work.[82]

When August took the girls to view this rich site, calling them hieroglyphics emphasized the exotic un-readability of the iconography of people whose territory the incomers claimed, but it also suggests there was something that could be read by the target audience that reflected their ideas about their environment and existence within it. Klahoose elder Ken Hanuse told me, "Our name for a single-headed serpent is 'yexa gija.' It had the head of a horse and a basket-like tail. Elder Lill Hill saw one that moved faster than a boat. I heard a 10-foot serpent was seen up in Bute by a Homalco man." The related Tla'amin People refer to Savary Island as a double-headed serpent called Ayhus.

Asked about the Orford picto complex, Homalco Chief Darren Blaney said, "The first Xwe'malhkwu man's name was Gee-thlmatun ('runs to him'). Because he couldn't say no to people who came to him, he was a respected leader.

"During his vision quests he went up to the high lakes in our territory. Like other seekers he would bathe, cut his legs and sweep his body with hemlock or cedar boughs as much as three times a day for up to seven years to get a spirit guide. Marianne Harry's grandfather went way up the Homathko to Tatlayoko Lake on such a vision quest. Some men training to hunt alpine goats learned from bears to eat hellebore to empty themselves and gain strength.

"During a vision quest a series of different guides would come. First might be a grouse, then a bear, or a salmon, which would bring fishing power, but they could go on up to the two-headed serpent, a teaching about leadership ability and making the right choice. The highest vision was the North Star. That was the medicine man.

"In his vision season, Gee-thlmatun, the eldest of the Dog Children, saw a two-headed serpent that showed him its powers. In a dancing power its two heads could be cut off, but it kept dancing until they touched and the body was healed. Way beyond the metaphysical, this power could bring physical results."

Darren feels the Orford pictos have something to do with a serpent vision, but such information was kept secret after contact, especially from the Catholic Church and Indian agents.[83]

People often ask if these pictographs are old. Without datable organic material the answer is that for the most part we do not know. A more trackable question might be, where do iconic Northwest Coast serpent forms come from? The Courtenay Museum on Vancouver Island holds the 6-metre (20-foot) fossil skeleton of an Elasmosaur, a local aquatic creature from the Late Cretaceous period. Indigenous people seeing such fossils might wonder if a sea serpent still haunted nearby waters when a similarly configured log streamed by on an outflow. The local wolf eel does resemble the bulging-headed Homfray pictograph. An impressive 2 to 2.5 metres (7 to 8 feet) long, and oddly curious, eels can be fed by divers, although they are capable of inflicting serious bites. Some Southern Salish Makah People caught wolf eels they called "Dr. Fish" at low tide in the summer months. The sweet/savoury flesh was eaten only by medicine men wishing to enhance their abilities.

In the Pacific Northwest the washed-up, stripped carcasses of the once-common basking shark, all head and 9-metre (30-foot) spine, have occasionally been reported as sea serpent remains. Ancient carvings of sea wolves on Quadra Island, at Petroglyph Park on Vancouver

Orford River humanoid pictograph.
Judith Williams photo

Island below Nanaimo, and far away in Prince Rupert notate the persistence of sea oddity images coastwide. Is the Sisiutl, Sillhqey or sea wolf, like ongoing imaging of dragons, based on the real crossed with the desired or feared or the extinct? What does it mean to reproduce such images through time? To what degree do we see what we are culturally taught to see, and how does that picturing affect how one is in the world?

The wonderful Orford rock art complex pictures a local Indigenous concept, event or belief. August and the girls depicted what was important in their life in film and words. It's popularly said that the first drawing was made by a girl tracing the shadow of her suitor on a wall to capture some essence of the departing lover. Photographing the beloved Leo as a semi-animate pelt after his death attempts to collapse time, but also endlessly repeats loss. To photograph Pearl hugging Girlie captures the cougar's unique relationship with the girls, and being photographed in such an unbelievable affectionate embrace with a wild creature defines the girls' uniqueness for us. Only later did Marion construct *Cougar Companions* to fix positive memories of that period for them. Like the pictographs, the Schnarr images become a theatre of their period in which a person or creature acts out the scene of the image in the memory of those depicted or depicting, and for us.

Gitxsan cougar image, Kitwanga, 1905.
"The Totem Poles and Monuments of Gitwangak Village," George F. MacDonald

The existent or nonexistent source of creatures portrayed in rock art opens the door on a curious absence. Considering the extensive representation of most coastal creatures in First Nations rock art, masks, poles and story, and the painted serpentine creatures in Toba and Bute, the dearth of clearly identifiable cougar imagery in Northwest Coast Indigenous art is fascinating. The largest and most aggressive population of cougars in the world was said to live on Vancouver Island until the government bounty program from the 1920s to the '50s, and they are still wonderfully on the prowl throughout the BC coast and into the Interior. Certainly August had little trouble finding them. Johnny Schnarr claimed that in their forays between Knight and Bute in 1910–12 they shot forty.

Most animals found in coastal BC territory are included in the Dance of the Animals given by certain Kwakwaka'wakw and Oweekino families to indicate the source and validation of family crests. Almost every creature except a cougar is called out by a Wolf or Grouse speaker to dance. Stories or recognizable representations of cougars from those or any other coastal group are almost nonexistent, and they are not normally considered a crest animal.

There are two Gitxsan exceptions. A 1910 photograph taken at Kitwanga in the BC Interior shows a wooden box surmounted by a cougar that wandered north and killed people in Skeena. The cougar was killed and taken by a Kitwanga clan as a crest. A Gitxsan pole shows a cougar at its top, surmounting a wolf.

Negotiating fog, rain and an invisible shoreline while boating southward from Orford Bay had a dampening effect on my fanciful speculation about the meanings of images. We needed to find real landmarks. I drove a compass course north–south to Lewis Channel along what had to be the west side of Raza Island, although it seemed to go on and on.

Suddenly Bobo said, "That's Redonda," and insisted I turn to port.

But wasn't that a house I knew to be *in* Redonda *Bay*? I turned away, west along the shore, found the small island at Redonda Bay's west mouth and rounded the north tip of West Redonda Island to the Redonda light at the top of Lewis Channel. When a faint shadow of Bullock Bluff, across the channel at the north end of Cortes Island, appeared, I scooted over from West Redonda to the Cortes shore and followed it along south, home to Squirrel Cove dock.

August 18. On the water again, at Channel Island off the mouth of Toba Inlet, we saw an enormous floating whale. What looked to be a small flesh-coloured log lay alongside it. Periodically the whale blew and rolled its massive, slightly ridged back forward in the sea to reveal a small sickle-shaped fin but never its tail. Suddenly, out from within the creature whooshed a red material containing bobbing, square, doughnut-shaped white forms.

Still and monstrous in size, the creature, when I reported it to the Wild Ocean Whale Society, answered to all the characteristics of a fin whale, the second-largest creature in the world. Fin and humpback whales, which once inhabited the Salish Sea, were wiped out in a handful of years by whalers from Blubber Bay on Texada Island and Whaletown on Cortes. Fin whales are reported to feed on the oily copepods scientists say bloom so abundantly in Bute, and a vet suggested the "doughnuts" might be undigested fat. The Orford "serpents" may derive from something passing that was as real and as surprising as Pearl hugging Girlie.

EPILOGUE

WHAT CAN YOU SEE IN A PHOTOGRAPH?

A handsome Mrs. Williams holds the head of a cougar propped up on the lopped-off end of a boomstick. August holds its tail.

The tide is out and the cougar is very dead. You can't see that Mrs. Williams was a follower of numerology and changed her name frequently. I mourn the cougar as Mrs. Williams and August do not. The photo dates from somewhere between the late 1930s and early 1940s. Where are they?

In 1973, Loughborough upcoasters Dane Campbell and Helen Piddington met August in his dusky Heriot Bay floathouse, like that propped up on pilings behind him in the photo. In his shed he showed them a rotary engine from a brand-new Mazda he was installing in his longboat. He calculated its unique configuration would provide superior power to drive the airboat propeller. August was friendly, Dane said, but cantankerous about game laws and the government. "He never mentioned his family, told stories about his days trapping up at the end of Bute and tried to sell me his old boom chains for an exorbitant $40 each." The Mazda sat unused for years.

"I went to that Heriot Bay shed once," August's great-granddaughter Kenna Fair told me. "Oh! It was full of tools and a boat he was building and never finished. There were cougar, wolf and bearskins all over, a great mass of things lost in what to me was a huge space. I don't remember the propellers. It was dark in there and I was very young. I wanted to make a film about them all, but by the time I talked to my grandmother Pansy she had Alzheimer's, and Great-Aunt Marion would not let me visit."[84]

My lined-out "Patience" suits of photographs and papers—the girls and their friends, a pleading letter, a live or a dead cougar—have come to resemble the elements of a Schnarr floathouse that disassemble and shift, become a film flickering through an ancient projector in a dim old community hall. The beam of light expanding from aperture to screen, filled with the grains of dust you seldom see, and the crackle of brittle sprocket holes breaking in old machinery fracture simple chronology or narrative, promote invention. As girls cajole cougars

Opposite: Mrs. Williams, August Schnarr and cougar. *August Schnarr negatives. Image MCR 8493 courtesy of the Museum at Campbell River*

Marion and Leo, c. 1937. *Schnarr family photo,* Cougar Companions *album. Image MCR 2006-8 courtesy of the Museum at Campbell River*

across snow to face the professional cameraman, Biddie Belton cringes, afraid, and I invent her visit. I find a picture of Daisy Walker and her child, years after she lived in Bute, and concoct for her a diary of the 1895 Chilko Lake trip, when the excruciatingly doomed horses were brought down the grease trail.

Time's current clusters and re-sorts meaning for me as my wonky taxonomy clanks through the light. Photographs can be analyzed by structuralist, social or psychological theories that can illuminate or obscure the people and eras depicted, but the edges of any such analysis I might have entertained have become ragged as they intersect with the memories of still-living subjects telling their versions of events and my own reading of and projection into the images.

I study the potent image of Marion, who will not now speak, and Leo, who could not. It actualizes what can never again be. Did two creatures from different species ever share such a direct and accessing glance at the same camera, at us? Close your eyes. Do you remember the chain or a glance? Do you think about a cocked elbow? What scenario do you create?

A girl raises one arm over her head and lies back against the settee: Marion in socks and slippers. Pansy stands bent over a table. She stops writing the diary four days after Marion's birthday, September 3, 1939. Leo had died. Tomorrow and tomorrow and tomorrow logs need to be boomed, traps checked, dinner cooked; the pig slaughtered, butchered, salted, canned; potatoes planted, hilled, dug, stored and fed to new pigs to slaughter. The work was endless. Marion only lounges in my head. How desperate were the girls?

Len comes to call. His ailing wife needs help. He can pay. Marion agrees. "We are just ordinary working people," she later wrote. At Bear Bay, under the stuffed sea lion head, the stove glows cherry red. Marion drops down in a chair. Mrs. Parker is dying. Did Len stand in the doorway and read from his poem "Marion Mountain Murmurs"? "I have mothered, fed and sheltered/ All of life that came to me."

I look at this photo of Marion and Leo in the late 1930s, at a faded Xerox of Len's face. How lonely did it get? Something happened. How old was he, how innocent she? Pansy said that when August was away, boys came to visit. I think about Gunner's box of chocolates. "Those old guys up there," Pearl said, "they took advantage of us."

When handsome young Lloyd Fair stopped in at the Schnarr floathouse from trapping up the Southgate in the late 1930s, he and Pansy looked at each other hopefully. At the end of her life she said, "I didn't know what it was to be a wife."

Sometimes I think that . . . I see Pearl taking money from a can up on a shelf, getting on the steamer alone. "Married a military man," she said. Then her Albert drowned. She married John Macklin, lived uphill from her father and had sons and a daughter, worked at the Wal Can fish cannery in Quathiaski Cove as long as they let her. When August died he cut Marion out of his will, but Pearl gave her half of what she received. Marion and Robert Tyrrell published *Rumrunner* in 1988, dedicated to "Alma Van der Est a second mother and a friend," who taught Marion to write and fed and supported her during her early years. When I asked Marion about her *Cougar Companions* albums she said, "I'm too old, I can't remember much, I don't want to go back."

A photo can frame just a section of a face or event, corrupt memory and skew meaning. Marion, in creating each slightly different album, organized recollection so the harshness of their lives is replaced by a vision of a life with a mother and the cougars, before August moved

Owen Bay school, Sonora Island, BC, 1935. Back row: Art Van der Est, Pearl Schnarr, Miss Sweetum (teacher), Marion Schnarr, John Van der Est. Front row: Len, Bill and Jim Van der Est.
Van der Est collection

them back to Bute, life split apart and three girls found the road to womanhood rocky. Was this how she let go?

In assembling the archival dossiers and laying images out in suits, I remade their past infused with my own formative engagement with this coast. Pansy's record of their house move is informed by my documentation of Ken MacPherson moving the last floathouse at Refuge Cove in 1988. I mine my childhood memories of Texada Island to construct a time when August smiled, before Zaida died. Here comes baby me crawling across a Blubber Bay lawn toward a cat, a "memory" that really only exists for me as a photo in my mother's family album.

August Schnarr died in 1981 at ninety-five.
Maud Emery collection

I am the fourth girl, just outside the *Cougar Companions'* frame, haunted by the image of Pearl hugging Girlie. I see love and trust, see a collar and chain. Moving right to left upstage in that photo is Marion who stayed up-inlet longest, moved through the bush, up the rivers and mountains, carried a gun and shot "hooters." "Marion was once confronted by a wolf," Pansy said, "and, of course, you want to shoot it and she did. Then, thinking she might just have wounded it, felt bad, felt afraid." I see that right through Pearl in 2010, bent over the image of her and Girlie, looking at herself planning to flee: "Not one more fight." I see it was hard. I fear the "backhander." How harsh was August? How fond were the memories?

When Pearl died she asked that her ashes be taken back to the site of their Owen Bay cabin. She told Glen that attending the school there, full of other children taught by Alma Van der Est, was the happiest time of her life. At first *Cougar Companions* made me think Leo and Girlie, devoted only to the girls, provided the psychological glue making other aspects of their hard life tolerable after Zaida died. But in Pansy's *Early Days* album I found a happy photo of the girls and their friend Frankie laughing, holding the octopus at Owen Bay. I see cheeky Van der Est boys laughing at Owen Bay school.

I have used the photographs in Marion's theatre of memory to construct and stage, on a magnificent and demanding set, a broader "Cougar Companions." It is a performance of astoundingly rich lives by remarkably strong individuals.

"WE TOOK HIS ASHES UP THERE, WE FIGURED HE WOULD LIKE THAT: HE WAS AN UNRELIGIOUS MAN."

—PANSY SCHNARR FAIR EDDINGTON

Endnotes

1 British Columbia, Ministry of Forests, Lands and Natural Resource Operations publication. From the collection of the University of British Columbia Library Rare Books and Special Collections, Vancouver, Canada.

2 August Schnarr tapes, interview by Joan Skogan and Jan Havelaar, February 15, 1977, #A028 1-3, Campbell River Museum. All of August's comments are from this interview unless otherwise indicated.

3 Judith Williams, *High Slack: Waddington's Gold Road and the Bute Inlet Massacre of 1864* (Vancouver: New Star Books, 1995).

4 These notebooks are now in the Campbell River Museum.

5 This would seem to be the cabin shown as Gus Schnarr's Bakery in photo at the top of page 49.

6 Maud Emery, "Never Believe Them When They Say 'It Can't Be Done,'" *Daily Colonist*, October 2, 1960.

7 Marion Parker and Robert Tyrrell, *Rumrunner: The Life and Times of Johnny Schnarr* (Victoria: Orca Books, 1988).

8 Emery, "Never Believe Them."

9 The term "fonds" originated in French archival practice. In Canada it has officially replaced the misleading term "collection," now only used for document aggregations assembled, but not created, by a collector.

10 Although this photo is in Pearl's *Cougar Companions* album, in the BC Archives and in the "Water Power Investigations" report, the original negative must be missing from the Museum at Campbell River Klinaklini Glacier set.

11 Imbert Orchard interview with Dennis Walker, 1965 (BC Archives); personal communication with Vern Logan, Dennis's grandson.

12 See Dorothy Kennedy and Randy Bouchard, *Sliammon Life, Sliammon Lands* (Vancouver: Talonbooks, 1983).

13 Information from Rankin's wife, Susan, and great-niece Anne Dewar.

14 From a story by Andy Ellingson. Private communication.

15 See Beth Hill, *Upcoast Summers* (Victoria: Horsdal & Schubart, 1985), for Barrow's photos.

16 M.Y. Williams, "Bute Inlet Wax," in *Transactions of the Royal Society of Canada*, vol. 51, series 3 (1957).

17 Kennedy and Bouchard, *Sliammon Life, Sliammon Lands*.

18 The full story is "Raven and the Wind-Maker," told by Homalco elder Noel George Harry, c. 1970s, in Kennedy and Bouchard, *Sliammon Life, Sliammon Lands*.

19 British Columbia, Ministry of Forests, Lands and Natural Resource Operations publication. From the collection of the University of British Columbia Library Rare Books and Special Collections, Vancouver, Canada.

20 Personal communication with John B.H. Edmond.

21 British Columbia, Ministry of Forests, Lands and Natural Resource Operations publication. From the collection of the University of British Columbia Library Rare Books and Special Collections, Vancouver, Canada.

22 British Columbia, Ministry of Forests, Lands and Natural Resource Operations publication. From the collection of the University of British Columbia Library Rare Books and Special Collections, Vancouver, Canada.

23 Don Munday, *The Unknown Mountain* (London: Hodder and Stoughton, 1948). After a number of tries by the Mundays, Fritz Wiessner and William House topped the mountain in 1936.

24 Quoted in Kathryn Bridge, *A Passion for Mountains: The Lives of Don and Phyllis Munday* (Victoria: Rocky Mountain Books, 2006).

25 From Jay Sherwood, ed., *Surveying Central British Columbia: A Photo Journal of Frank Swannell, 1920–28* (Victoria: Royal BC Museum, 2007).

26 Quoted in a 1978 letter by Dorothy McAuley in the Cortes Island Museum and Archives. Dorothy McAuley, a friend of Rasmussen's, was raised on Twin Islands.

27 See Williams, *High Slack*, 79.

28 British Columbia, Ministry of Forests, Lands and Natural Resource Operations publication. From the collection of the University of British Columbia Library Rare Books and Special Collections, Vancouver, Canada.

29 Munday, *The Unknown Mountain*.

30 A small, energetic, agile and fierce critter living in northern deciduous forests, the pine marten (genus *Martes* within the *Mustelinae* sub-family of *Mustelidae*) has a silky brownish pelt with a large bushy tail, and paws with partially retractable claws. Omnivorous relatives of wolverines, mink, ferrets and weasels, they eat squirrels, mice, birds, fish, insects, eggs and occasionally nuts and berries. The 2013 pelt price was $46 to $80.

31 A version of Charlie's diary was made for the *Naming and Claiming: The Creation of Bute Inlet* exhibition, with Sylvia Ives's permission.

32 Charles Blondin, born Jean François Gravelet, was famous for walking a tightrope across Niagara Falls in 1859.

33 Story told to me by Darren Blaney, Homalco Chief.

34 Ulloa, named after the Battle of Ulloa by the Spanish, became known as Twin Islands after the Andrewses' launch *Twin Isles*.

35 Bill Thompson, *Once Upon a Stump* (Powell River: Powell River Heritage Research Association, 1993).

36 Adrian Kershaw and John Spittle, *The Bute Inlet Route: Alfred Waddington's Wagon Road, 1862–1864* (Kelowna: Okanagan College, 1978).

37 Information from a letter Len Parker wrote to Adrian Redford in Lund in 1983 when he and Laurette were living in Victoria.

38 Maud Emery, "Pouncing Pets," *Daily Colonist*, October 23, 1964; Pansy Schnarr tapes, Aural interview # A22, 1-2, Campbell River Museum.

39 From *Cougar Companions*.

40 Pansy Schnarr Eddington tapes, Campbell River Museum.

41 Pansy Schnarr Eddington tapes, Campbell River Museum.

42 "Looking Back," *Musings*, Vol. 2 (July 1991), CRMA.

43 "Looking Back," *Musings*, Vol. 2 (July 1991), CRMA.

44 Emery, "Pouncing Pets."

45 Publisher's description of Susan Howe, *Spontaneous Particulars: The Telepathy of Archives* (New York: New Directions, 2014).

46 Pansy Schnarr Eddington tapes, Campbell River Museum.

47 I have reluctantly edited Pansy's diary (CRMA) but have hopefully left her voice intact.

48 Len Parker "Resume," included with Laurette Parker's letter to the Margrave von Baden and family, September 14, 1987, after Len's death.

49 From Elizabeth Hawkins, *Jack Mould and the Curse of Gold* (Surrey, BC: Hancock House, 1993)

50 Judith Williams, *Dynamite Stories* (Vancouver: New Star Books, 2003).

51 British Columbia, Ministry of Forests, Lands and Natural Resource Operations publication. From the collection of the University of British Columbia Library Rare Books and Special Collections, Vancouver, Canada.

52 Judith Williams, *Clam Gardens: Aboriginal Mariculture on Canada's West Coast* (Vancouver: New Star Books, 2006).

53 From *A Spanish Voyage to Vancouver and the Northwest Coast of America*, trans. Cecil Jane (London: Argonaut, 1930).

54 Whymper's drawings, engraved for his *Illustrated London News* story about the 1864 Homathko events, were later published in *Travels and Adventures in the Territory of Alaska* (London: J. Murray, 1868).

55 See Williams, *High Slack*.

56 Klatsassine, the name of the war chief who allegedly led the attack on the Waddington road crew, can be translated as "nobody knows his name." See Williams, *High Slack*, and Stan Douglas's film *Klatsassin* (2006).

57 There were routes up from Bear River to the Apple River Valley in Loughborough Inlet, and from Bute up the Orford toward the Tuhumming River in Toba.

58 British Columbia, Ministry of Forests, Lands and Natural Resource Operations publication. From the collection of the University of British Columbia Library Rare Books and Special Collections, Vancouver, Canada.

59 British Columbia, Ministry of Forests, Lands and Natural Resource Operations publication. From the collection of the University of British Columbia Library Rare Books and Special Collections, Vancouver, Canada.

60 Parker and Tyrrell, *Rumrunner*.

61 Heather Kellerhals, personal communication.

62 BC Parks Division: Cariboo District, *Tŝ'il?os Provincial Park Master Plan* (Victoria: BC Parks, 1997), 13.

63 Eulachon oil is known for its relatively high docosahexaenoic acid (DHA) content, with a remarkable 1,500 per cent increase after ripening and rendering. DHA repairs and builds material for brain nerve synapses and is involved with replacing the sticky surface of blood cells with a slippery coating to reduce the tendency of the cells to clog the arterial system.

64 Nigel Haggan and Associates, "The Case for Including the Cultural and Spiritual Value of Eulachon in Policy and Decision-Making" (report prepared for Fisheries and Oceans Canada, 2010).

65 Homer G. Barnett, *The Coast Salish of British Columbia* (Portland: University of Oregon Press, 1955).

66 Randy Bouchard and Dorothy Kennedy, private communication.

67 See Richard F. Lee, "Lipids of Zooplankton from Bute Inlet, British Columbia," *Journal of the Fisheries Research Board of Canada*, 31 (2011): 1577–1582. doi 10.1139/f74-198 (www.researchgate.net/publication/237179637).

68 T.C. Jain and T.J. Striha, "Studies Related to Bute Wax: The Identity of Norphytane, Pristane and Bute Hydrocarbon," *Canadian Journal of Chemistry* 47, no. 23 (1969): 4359–4361. Although there has been little recent Canadian study of Bute wax, there are marine oil investigations in Finland. Also see R.F. Lee, W. Hagen, and G. Kattner, "Lipid Storage in Marine Zooplankton," *Marine Ecology Progress Series* 307 (2006): 273–306.

69 Williams, *High Slack*.

70 Richard F. Lee and J.C. Nevenzel, "Wax Esters in the Marine Environment: Origin and Composition of the Wax from Bute Inlet, British Columbia," *Journal of the Fisheries Research Board of Canada*, 36 (1979): 1519–1523.

71 Their optimism is heartening, but the Homalco salmon hatchery at Orford Bay was damaged when the BC Forests Ministry allowed logging directly above a creek feeding into its new fish tanks.

72 From "The Slide," Arne Liseth, Friends of Bute Inlet website, buteinlet.net.

73 Material about the court case in the Schnarr fonds, Campbell River Museum.

74 Quoted in Kennedy and Bouchard, *Sliammon Life, Sliammon Lands*.

75 See *The Man Who Can Fly* (produced by Reel Water Productions for *National Geographic* Channel, 2011), shot in Bute Inlet. Potter died in May 2015.

76 I sent the GPS location to Doris Lundy at the BC Archaeology office for inclusion in their files. Doris sent back its Bordon number, EdSf-3, which now identifies the site.

77 Private communication from Randy Bouchard.

78 P.B. McCall and D.E. Hay, "Distribution of Spawning Eulachon Stocks in the Central Coast of British Columbia as Indicated by Larval Surveys," Department of Fisheries and Oceans Canada, Canadian Stock Assessment Secretariat Document 99/177 (1999), www.dfo-mpo.gc.ca/Library/242316.pdf.

79 Stuart's house in Berkeley Square was later bought by W. Petty Fitzmaurice, 1st Marquess of Lansdowne.

80 From Hawkins, *Jack Mould and the Curse of Gold*, Hancock.

81 Judith Williams, *Two Wolves at the Dawn of Time: Kingcome Inlet Pictographs, 1893–1998* (Vancouver: New Star Books, 2001).

82 Judith Williams, *Two Wolves at the Dawn of Time: Kingcome Inlet Pictographs, 1893–1998* (Vancouver: New Star Books, 2001).

83 Information from Jeanette Taylor interview, 2008, and from private 2018 communication with Darren Blaney, who cites Homalco elder Ambrose Wilson as his source.

84 Although the man in the photograph is identified as "Schnarr," there is a slight possibility it is August's neighbour Dougie Dowler, the owner of the Heriot Bay store.

Index

Page numbers in bold refer to photographs, illustrations and maps.